STELLA ADLER
THE ART OF ACTING

▼

STELLA ADLER
THE ART OF ACTING

▼

COMPILED & EDITED BY
HOWARD KISSEL

APPLAUSE

An Applause Original
THE ART OF ACTING by Stella Adler
Compiled and edited by Howard Kissel
Copyright © 2000 by Applause Books
Afterword copyright © 2000 by Howard Kissel
All rights reserved. Printed in Canada

Jacket and frontispiece photos courtesy of Irene Gilbert, Archival Collection, Stella Adler Academy and Theatre–Los Angeles

ISBN 1-55783-373-7

Library of Congress Cataloging-in-Publication Data
Library of Congress Card Number: 00-108803

British Library Cataloging-in-Publication Data

A catalogue record for this book is available from the British Library.

Applause Theatre & Cinema Books
19 West 21st Street, Suite 201
New York, NY 10010
Phone: (212) 575-9265
Fax: (212) 575-9270
Email: info@applausepub.com
Internet: www.applausepub.com

Applause books are available through your local bookstore, or you may order at www.applausepub.com or call Music Dispatch at 800-637-2852.

Sales & Distribution:

North America:
Hal Leonard Corp.
7777 West Bluemound Road
P.O. Box 13819
Milwaukee, WI 53213
Phone: (414) 774-3630
Fax: (414) 774-3259
Email: halinfo@halleonard.com
Internet: www.halleonard.com

Europe:
Roundhouse Publishing Ltd.
Millstone, Limers Lane
Northam, North Devon
EX 39 2RG
Phone: 01237-474474
Fax: 01237-474774
Email: roundhouse.group@ukgateway.net

CONTENTS

Preface

To me Stella Adler is much more than a teacher of acting. Through her work she imparts the most valuable kind of information — how to discover the nature of our own emotional mechanics and therefore those of others. She never lent herself to vulgar exploitations, as some other well-known so-called "methods" of acting have done. As a result, her contributions to the theatrical culture have remained largely unknown, unrecognized, and unappreciated.

As far as I know, she was the only American artist who went to Paris to study with Konstantin Stanislavski, who was himself a skilled observer of human behavior and a most prominent figure in Russian theatre. She brought back to this country a knowledge of his technique and incorporated it in her teaching. Little did she know that her teachings would impact theatrical culture worldwide. Almost all filmmaking anywhere in the world has been affected by American films, which has been, in turn, influenced by Stella Adler's teachings. She is loved by many and we owe her much.

I am grateful to the inestimable contributions she has made to my life and I feel privileged to have been associated with her and her family professionally and personally throughout my life.

— MARLON BRANDO

FIRST STEPS ON STAGE

O ver the next few months you will hear me say repeatedly that acting is not about *you*. But right at the start I want you to know that you do matter.

You live in a very busy world. You didn't have your coffee, or you grabbed it at the cafeteria. Your baby is home crying, or your husband doesn't love you, or your boyfriend didn't call you. Everybody has troubles.

Then there's the scattered person who doesn't know where she is. She's late for no reason. She's just late. That's her way of life.

You must understand that while you're in this room you leave the outside world outside. You need all of *yourself* here. You don't need your father. You don't need your mother. You don't need your husband. You don't need your child. You don't care what happens in *The New York Times*.

You need 100 percent honorable selfishness toward *you*.

▼

You are about to embrace a profession that is 2,000 years old. However, what being an actor has meant for most of that time is not what it means now.

Actors today face certain requirements, certain realities that would have been unheard of, even impossible fifty years ago. People would have been astonished at an actress being required to audition for Juliet, for instance. When I was a young actress you didn't audition. You were a member of a company, and they'd seen you. They had practically raised you.

They wouldn't dream of producing *Romeo and Juliet* unless they were sure they had, right in their company, a capable Romeo, a capable Juliet, a good Nurse, a good Friar Laurence. They had seen you develop as an actor over a period of time. They knew what you could do. And what you couldn't.

You joined the company, and you traveled through the provinces. You played little parts. That's how you learned to act. They showed you how to hold a spear. They saw you weren't holding it right and they showed you how to hold it. That's how you learned to hold a spear and, eventually, how to play Hamlet.

You're not so lucky. You only think you are, because you've been fed dreams of actors being "discovered" at drug store counters. But even if that dream *did* come true, if you shot right to the top, you'd be the poorer actor for never learning how to hold that spear. And you'd never know why either.

Carrying a spear makes you a different person. You have to see what it means to carry a spear at that time. Today there's no reason to carry a spear. Or no longer the same reason. In other times there were extremely important reasons for it, and for doing it right. Was it for a great ceremony? Was it for warfare? You must understand those reasons. This is the essence of our job as actors.

Today you can start not holding the spear but on top. Today we have instant actors. You can start by being the lead. You can start anywhere they want you to start. This is an absolutely new phenomenon.

Nobody took you out of a drugstore and said, "Play D'Artagnan." You were in a company. You played a young man. Maybe you played an old man. You played a little comedy, a little drama. Nobody who played Falstaff could also play Romeo. By being in such a company everyone found his scale.

Today's actors don't have this priceless resource. You and your scale are an unknown quantity. The only way you can learn your scale, that you can learn your job quickly — because that is what acting demands of you today — is through a studio, a school.

Now there is a certain snobbism today that says you don't learn acting by . . . acting. They think you *have* to learn acting in a classroom. Well, I learned acting by acting. But that's over. There are people who travelled the country by covered wagon. That's over too. The classroom is not ideal, but it's all you have. And so here you are.

You're here to learn a tradition that goes back two millenia. The theatre has roots that go back to Ancient Greece. The stream of dramatic literature runs from the Roman to the Elizabethan, to the Jacobean, to the Restoration, to the French Renaissance, to the Romantic Period, to Ibsenian Realism and Naturalism and leading to the gulf of the 20th Century. The tradition embraces all the regional and national characteristics, all the languages, all the shifting, changing styles, the different periods of time, the different levels of society, the mores and morals of passing years . . . the cut of clothing from generation to generation . . . the different furnitures, the very sound of the music in the air, the evolution that has changed the earthenware mug into a paper drinking cup.

This is the inheritance of the actor, the theatre student of today.

It's an awful lot of words to use to the actor, but somehow he must be made aware. The young actor today tends to be little. He seeks to protect his little emotion as he sits comfortably in his little chair in his little blue jeans and stares at his little world that extends from right to left.

He has confined himself to the beat of his generation only, bounded himself within the limits of his street corner and alienated himself from every object or period that doesn't contain *his* pulse.

The result of this is a disrespect for the world in general and a foreignness to anything around him that isn't immediately recognizable to his everyday habits. He has even begun to lose perspective on what his own assets and faults are, because he has nothing to measure these things against.

It is time to take the blindfold off.

▼

You come from different parts of society, from different neighborhoods. The thing that leads you here, at this moment, is that you have talent. Take my word for it. The thing that makes you say, "I want to do something" — that is the beginning of talent.

What is important and what you must always remember is that you had the courage to find the way, the grown-up sense to call up, to fill out an application, to find your way down here to me. Now say, "I have one credit on my side." Don't give that up for anybody. It is something you have done.

In your society, where they tear down old buildings and put up new ones, many of you are going to aim at making money. Even if you started becoming a priest, somehow you're going to try to cash in on it. I've never asked a priest about this, but someday I will. These different aims are in you. It's what your mother thinks, your father thinks. Everybody tells you that you have to be successful. Success means for some of you TV, movies, working all the time. It means being applauded. It means being reassured.

I'll let you in on a big secret. No actor is a success unless he feels inside himself, as long as he lives, that he is good. If you don't feel that you're good, no money can give it to you! No applause can give it to you! No symbol of success can give it to you! That feeling, of an artist or an actress, that confidence must come from him in spite of everything. And this is the confidence we must establish in you. And when you have it, you will not need me. You will not need anybody. You will *collaborate* with the director, but you will never say, "Help me!"

▼

An actress must be secure. You must travel 10,000 miles to find the person who gives you a technique that makes you secure. You have to keep growing in order to feel secure. You must not have an aim that is low. You cannot have an aim that is low and keep your security. Security when you get it gives you growth. The doctor who doesn't grow in his science is a hack. The actor that doesn't grow is a hack.

Write this down: "My aim is to be independent from Miss Adler or anybody else. I know this as well as you do, and in the sense that I know it as well as you do, I don't need you." And I will help you to achieve this independence.

▼

I have had people walk up to me and ask, "Do you teach The Method?" or "Are you 'Method'?"

Now Mr. Stanislavsky himself — and I'll tell you this with great pride, as I'm the only person I know who actually worked with him — Mr. Stanislavsky himself was a very conservative teacher.

If you read his book you will see this. But don't read his book, because it absolutely makes no sense. He came from a culture entirely alien to yours, and you won't understand it. He spends the whole time talking in his second book and his third book about the beauty of a vowel and what "s" means and how "s" can mean five million things. You'll only get confused. He was very busy with things that have nothing to do with the so-called interpretation of The Method.

Mr. Stanislavsky had *his* Method. Do you understand? It was a method that included the French style of acting, which was based on Commedia dell'Arte. It was a method that included the Italian school of operatic acting. For Stanislavsky the greatest actor was Salvini, and Salvini said, "What is acting? Voice. Voice. And Voice." This is what Mr. Stanislavsky also included.

The Method is something you'll find through me. I am one of the two million people who have been inspired by it. But my particular contribution will be to make you *independent* of The Method. You will then have the strength to reformulate it and go your own way.

Nowadays it's very fashionable to be a Method actor. Therefore it's time to change. When it's really fashionable, there's something wrong.

An actor once came up to me and said, "I'm a Meth. . ." and he mumbled something. I said, "Get out of here. I don't want that around. It's too corrupt."

▼

You won't have the chance to learn this ten times in your life. You're lucky because I come from the same society that you come from. The society did not swallow me. It didn't eat me up. It tried to, but I came out and in some way you will too.

I know you must make a living, and I know you must be a success. I know that in our society we can't pretend success doesn't matter. But beyond that you must understand that soon you'll have in front of you a picture of your whole self, a diagnostic photograph.

And this photograph will say, "This is what I am capable of, and this is what I must work on. The success and the money will then be in proportion to what you can become. You must consider at each juncture, "Am I willing to trade this much work and progress for this much success and money? (And at times the money and success will be zero.)

Today the influences of your society pressure you to be successful before your time. They are pulling you down. They have pulled you down, you big, sweet, magnificent, young, potential artists. They have pulled you down so far that you are on the verge of destruction. Only you don't know it because you want to be a success.

I want you to be able to say, "They can give me the part or they can take away the part. I know I'm an actress. I know how to live with my work, whether or not they give me the part. I know without them giving me the chance.

How do I do that? How would I do that? Because I would never have thought of going into a commercial play if I could play in a good theatre. I knew the great people — Mr. Stanislavsky, Mr. Guthrie, Mr. Reinhardt. They don't aim as low as most managers. I needed their respect. If you say, "I want to go on TV," then if they take TV away from you what will you do? How will you survive? If they take TV away from Mr. Guthrie, he is still Mr. Guthrie. Reinhardt, too.

I would say, for every dollar you want to make in the theatre, say, "I want and will find out how to live and work without that dollar." For every hour you spend trying to make money in the theatre, put in an hour's work somewhere. That hour will be for yourself.

You will not only be paid back with money, but with growth, with opportunity to survive, to be without the outside sense of success but with the inside ability to grow. If you learn how to work and grow, you will find that your life cannot be destroyed by the outside world. If you have to work eight hours a day, give three or one that belongs to you without money. This "Who Are You?" has to be reinforced.

At the end of work with me you must be able to say, "My life belongs to me, no matter where I am." You must not fail because somebody out there doesn't give you a job. And the way not to fail is that for every hour you spend making money you must find a way that will help you. Your destiny is to divide your time up for a while. This is the difference between wanting to play a part and having a way of life that includes the part.

Even if you're swallowed up by the aim of being a success — and you may be — this training will help you because you will always know what you must bring to any experience in the theatre.

Otherwise they'll give you success and you'll be successful, and when they take the success away you'll fail. Ah, it's too precarious for life. You must be in control of everything as long as you live. And since you are an actor, that is what you must be in control of.

I will help you stretch yourself, but your aim must be clear to you first.

▼

Your first assignment is to write down what your aim is. You might write, "My aim is to get brightness out of the theatre and laughter and fun. For this I need dancing and a body that moves. I'm going to learn to sing. I need to learn music. I need to learn how to deal with all the things that are comedy, that are fast, that are good, that require my entire equipment for all time. That means not only for now, but for some time when I do Gilbert and Sullivan."

You will quickly see that to achieve your true dimension you have to stretch, you have to expand. To speak on stage you can't use your everyday speech. It doesn't work. The stretch is a great privilege. Only the artist is responsible for stretching. It's entirely up to you. And it isn't easy. But when the artist does stretch, the entire world limbers up.

▼

When I began I told you you were permitted a certain kind of selfishness, a selfishness that focuses on the work. You must come here with a sense of quiet. You can't do that if you forget something — where's my book? Do I have a phone call?

I demand quiet. Get rid of everything. Get rid of the newspaper. Get rid of the pocketbook. Get rid of the lipstick. If you do you'll find a weight has been taken off you.

If you like, you can mix your dates up. You can even doublecross people on the outside. You can say you can't go to a party because . . . I don't care. But you can't miss a class. Don't for any reason, except death, stay away from class. Don't get a cold. Don't get a backache, and don't go to your psychoanalyst. It doesn't belong in the theatre.

You must have 100 percent health. You have to be healthy and know that you are. Actors don't sneeze on the stage. They don't catch pneumonia. They don't get chills. They don't itch, and their feet don't hurt them. They don't have lumbago. Nothing happens to them.

Health is something you owe yourself and your profession. I've been an actress all my life and I've never had a headache. You must not give in. This must be the one area in your life that is totally controlled.

Any faults you may have must be taken care of by yourself. I'm not going to go home and nurse you, and nobody else will. You have to know your faults and correct them. Mr. Stanislavsky had a bad lisp. When I worked with him in Paris, he said, "I cannot see you in the morning. I've got to work on my lisp for two hours." This was a man in his seventies, the head of the Moscow Art Theatre, two years before he died. He knew he had this problem, and he worked on it. Everybody here has work to do. It is a privilege to have this opportunity to work.

If your body is not in good shape or your voice is not in good shape, your acting cannot be in good shape. Do you understand? It is held in as if you were locked up and couldn't move. It's not that you can't act. It's that nine-tenths of you is locked up in this prison.

▼

In a time of great disorder, order is the one thing that will save your life. Students of acting could not have chosen a profession that is more orderly, for the curtain must go up at eight, and you have to be there precisely on time.

Casualness is not helpful to the actor in his work. I have seen acting students in Russia stand up when the teacher enters the room. As artists, they preserve a formality about themselves dictated by a sense of tradition. If you are introduced to a young student in Russia, he bows over your hand. When the visitor is singled out and made to feel special, the special nature of the theatre is once again affirmed.

If you insist on being casual all day long you will finally become uncaring. In *Heartbreak House*, Shaw created a daughter who placated herself so much that she ended by having no heart. Rather than adopting the casual attitude, you do better to lose yourself in giving and risk the mistake. By making an effort you will find your mind, heart and soul, and you will gain in confidence.

▼

What I am after is your best. You have to understand your best. Your best isn't Barrymore's best or Olivier's best or my best, but your own. Every person has his norm. And in that norm every person is a star. Olivier could stand on his head and still not be you. Only you can be you.

What a privilege! Nobody can reach what you can if you do it. So do it. We need your best, your voice, your body. We don't need for you to imitate anybody, because that would be *second* best. And second best is no better than your worst.

If you were here to study dance, the class would be about your legs. If you were here to study piano, it would be about the instrument. The actor uses his legs. He uses his voice, his eyes, his hands. He uses every part of his body. His body is his instrument.

The actor is totally exposed. He stands on the stage. He stands in the spotlight. His every movement is scrutinized. There's no place to hide. If you feel like hiding, you've come to the wrong place. Everything the actor does has consequence. There are no "throwaway" lines. Every line is laid down like track of the Orient Express.

The actor has to develop his body. The actor has to work on his voice. But the most important thing the actor has to work on is his mind.

▼

Nowadays a lot of what passes for acting is nothing more than finding yourself in some character. That doesn't interest me. Of course you have to bring your own experience to bear on the characters you play, but you have to realize right from the outset that Hamlet was not "a guy like you."

The theatre I grew up in was a place where actors did not want just to play themselves, as so many actors want to do today. They didn't want just to play characters different from themselves either. They wanted to play characters bigger than themselves.

In our theatre the actors often don't raise themselves to the level of the characters. They bring the great characters down to their level. I'm afraid we live in a world that celebrates smallness. Am I exaggerating? Yes. Are there exceptions? Of course. Many exceptions? No.

There was a time when to play Oedipus you had to be an important actor. Until thirty or forty years ago to play any major role, whether it was Hamlet or Willy Loman, you had to have size. Write this down: You have to develop size. That is what we are here to work on.

When you approach a big writer you must live up to what is big in him. You must take the measure of the writer's size, and find that stature and dimension in yourself. I come back to the word size. Acting has to do with size. It's the name of the game.

▼

There are a lot of things about acting that are easy to understand. A lot of actors grasp quite readily what to do with their voices, what they can achieve with their bodies. Some of the exercises you will do may strike you as mechanical, but I assure you they are only as mechanical as you want to make them. They all point toward something larger.

Your job isn't merely to do the exercise but to do it in the sense of something larger than the exercise. Either you learn to respect each exercise as if it were the opening night at La Scala or opening night at La Scala will be nothing more than an exercise. Do you see?

A certain amount of what we do as actors is totally within our control. Technique is first of all a way of controlling what we do on stage. It's also a way of helping us reach something deeper, something less tangible, something more difficult, which we must learn to wrestle to the ground.

Laurence Olivier used to talk about the moment when he had finished putting on his makeup and had adjusted his costume. He would take one last look in the mirror before leaving his dressing room. Sometimes, he would say, when he took that quick look, he didn't feel he was seeing himself in makeup and costume. Sometimes he had the eery sense that what he saw in the mirror was his character looking back at him.

One night, when Olivier was playing Othello, he gave what must have been an electrifying performance. Even he was startled by it. And the audience would not stop applauding. Maggie Smith, who was playing Desdemona, was also stunned. When the curtain was rung down for the last time, instead of going to her own dressing room she went to his. She found him sitting there alone in the dark.

"Larry," she asked him. "How did you do it?"

"I don't know," he said. "I don't know."

Olivier had great technique. Sometimes we Americans have too high a regard for English technique. And sometimes we feel that technique is all that they have, that they lack the kind of raw emotion we are oversupplied with. You don't give the kind of performance Olivier must have given that night without technique, without huge ambition, but you also have to have great stature.

Interestingly, shortly after giving this momentous performance Olivier went into a horrible artistic funk. I suppose it's what they would call a midlife crisis, but it was unusually severe. He was convinced he knew nothing about acting.

He was afraid every time he went out on stage that a moment would come in the performance when he would have to step down to the footlights, beg the audience's forgiveness and ask that the curtain be brought down because he would not be able to remember his lines or not be able to perform.

That never happened, but for years the possibility that it *might* happen haunted him. Many years afterward he described this crisis in an interview, and I wondered if it had to do with that night when he did some of the best acting he ever did in his life and didn't understand how.

In any event that's not a kind of acting we're used to seeing nowadays. I would go so far as to say we're afraid of that kind of acting. As I've said, we live in a world that celebrates smallness. But the platform you stand on is large. The author is large. Only you are small. Until now.

Let me give you a simple example. You can say two plus two equals four and make it seem quite unremarkable. You can also say two plus two equals four in a way that reveals that it is an idea that took millions of years to evolve. That's what we have to convey as actors. That's what requires size.

▼

I have a Most Wanted poster I'm going to bring in. For the most dangerous actor in New York. This actor is a killer. Do not take a single step toward his pedestrian world. This actor kills language. He kills ideas because he makes them common. In our world the actor has become the smallest element in the theatre. I want you to make him again the strongest element in the theatre.

I will help you develop habits that will give you size. We'll start with the way you speak. Your vocal quality needs development. It's all right for television, but it's not big enough for the theatre. When you stand on stage you must have a sense that you are addressing the whole world, and that what you say is so important the whole world must listen.

You're not speaking to the world in your own voice. You're speaking in the voice of an author who matters to the world, who's changed the world, not merely passed through it. We must work to decrease the disparity between the language you use every day and the language of important writers.

Don't be merely vernacular. Don't imitate the street. Don't use the language of bums. That's the language the actor on the Most Wanted poster relies upon. Get off that street. Don't associate with that actor. You have a very small idea of what "real life" is. You have to get beyond that.

▼

The theatre exists on words. It exists on the literary quality of language. I want you to think about the way you speak. I'm not asking you to take care with other people's words, but to care about your own words. What this means is that you have to edit yourself. You have to be disciplined. We have to learn to speak precisely. I want you to be articulate about your thoughts.

We have to learn the correct way to eat. Eating is a tremendously good thing to correct. Americans are obsessed about eating. On *The New York Times* bestseller list ten out of twelve books are on diet. None is about literature.

Nowadays people drink too much. It mistreats the body. The actor can't do that. He has to correct himself.

The business of editing yourself is a life task. It's not about auditions or being in rehearsal. I, for instance, am very strict about what I eat and I'm equally strict about what I read. You couldn't make me even pick up a book I don't want to read — any more than I'd drink a bottle of vodka for breakfast because somebody put it out on the table.

How many people read without aim? How many people read simply for amusement? You're too old for that. Reading is not for play. It is to gain knowledge. You don't ride a tricycle any more, do you? It's time for Dante, not Mother Goose.

My late husband, Mitchell Wilson, was a scientist. He and Enrico Fermi worked together on the development of the atomic bomb. My husband used to say that in our time ten years had been added to life. But not at the end. We didn't add the ten years to maturity. We added them to adolescence. We're still "kids" when we're 28.

I'm not telling you to give up innocence. We're here to train your innocence, to preserve it, to polish it. But don't confuse innocence with adolescence. I want you to be innocent, wise and ninety-five.

▼

There is one rule to be learned. Life is not you. Life is outside you. If it is outside, you must go toward it. You must go toward a person, and if he or she backs off it's their fault. The essential thing to know is that life is in front of you. Go toward it.

You may have been corrupted into thinking that you are important. If so you are a lost creature waiting for the world to come to you. An actress's whole life can be ruined if she expects life to come to her. Tell yourself that the world is outside, that it's not to be hidden from you, that you are going to thrust yourself forward and be relaxed in the world. You have chosen a field where you're going to be hurt to the blood. But to retreat from the pain is death.

▼

Let's talk about you and me now, about how we're going to work together. This is not a course for compliments. If you want to know how great you are, stay home and audition for your mother. I don't compliment myself and I'm certainly not going to compliment you.

You can be afraid of me, afraid of the stage, of the audience. Fear can upstage your career. You can play supporting roles to Fear your whole life. Is that what you want? You can say, "I'm afraid of her and I don't know why. Maybe it's because I'm afraid of authority."

Well, you have to tell yourself you're no longer a child and there is no Authority. You must not retreat into the selfish, crippled idea that "She scares me." Or the director scares me. Or the critic petrifies me. You have to say, "Miss Adler, I want to be afraid of you, but I won't be — because it's stupid. You're not holding a gun."

At times I will be angry with you. You mustn't take it personally. It's not about you personally, and it's not about me personally. It's about the work. I want you to care as much as I do.

I have heard it said that I terrify my students. I know what they mean, but I don't find that accurate. It's true that you may become terrified in this class. But I won't be terrifying you. You'll be terrifying yourselves. You may become terrified by how much you have to learn. And that sort of terror is a blessing — when you're nineteen or twenty-six. But postpone that terror until you're thirty-six — now, that's more than a terror, it's a tragedy.

▼

I want you to read *The Prophet* by Kahlil Gibran. Gibran was born in Lebanon in 1883, the grandson of a Maronite priest. When he was twelve his family moved to Boston, but after a few years he asked to be sent back to Lebanon, where he studied at a Maronite school in Beirut. After his studied he traveled all over the Middle East. He returned to the West and spent a few years in Paris where he studied under the great sculptor Rodin, who predicted a great future for him as an artist. Until his death in 1931 he produced many works combining the wisdom of both East and West, the most famous of which is *The Prophet*.

I want you to take one of his ideas, paraphrase it, write it out in your own words, then come back here, stand on the stage and give it to us.

This means you are dealing with a text, dealing with ideas. There is no such thing as a text without ideas. You will read it and read it and it will begin to make sense to you. The reason I give you Gibran is that he is able to lift you to where he wants to go. Your mind is inclined towards the pedestrian, but he wants to lift you to his level.

I don't want to baby you, but I have to because most of you have not had an education that has prepared you for the theatre. Ideas are difficult because they are on paper, but if you read them several times slowly, the ideas will become yours and you'll be able to give them back.

Nothing is stronger than The Idea — not Stella, not anybody, not even God.

The whole thing about acting is to give. The actor must above everything be generous. He doesn't hoard his riches. He has to say, "I want you to hear this essay. It has wonderful ideas."

But before you can be giving and magnanimous, you must have something to give. Ideas don't come from your legs. They don't come from your voice. They come from your mind. The theatre is built on developing your mind. It's an education for your mind. You can dance without a mind. You certainly can sing without a mind, but you can't act.

Dancing eliminates thinking. You have to understand I'm not a dancing teacher. You will have to concentrate your body in order to use your mind. Miss Adler isn't here to help you look or sound good. This is not Dale Carnegie.

▼

I want you to start making a habit of looking at things and writing down what you liked, what you disliked. I want you to do this every day. We can start right here. I like the color of the dress Miss Adler is wearing. I don't like her earrings — they're a little vulgar. I like that beautiful leather briefcase the boy in the first row has.

After a few weeks I want you to start adding why you liked what you liked. You'll find that you may like broken pavements, maybe because you think they're charming. Or you'll find you don't like broken pavements because you like things to have their own definable shape. You'll begin to discover things about your perceptions and your tastes.

I want you to bring in ten white objects, ten blue objects and ten red objects you will have seen this week — the red, for example, on that girl's sweater, or the blue on the book that boy has put under his chair.

There's one thing that exceeds all others: the eyes of the actor. If he sees, he sees specifically. He doesn't generalize. He must be careful. He must learn to see the difference between different reds — the red of a racing car, the red of a hibiscus, and the red of blood. They're three different reds. They mean three different things.

The ability to see specifically has to do with the ability to react differently. You don't respond to one red the way you do to another. You can respond passively to a red fire hydrant whose paint has faded and is streaked with off-white. You don't respond passively to the gleaming red of a fire engine whizzing by.

Critical seeing, self-awareness, discipline and self-control — these are the demands we'll be working on. But none of these, once mastered, will matter at all without the energy. You must develop the energy necessary for the stage. You have to work for it. God doesn't just give it to you.

The world is in front of you. You have to take it in. You have to see things you never saw before. Then you have to give it back to the world.

Everything you do as an actor is important. You have to feel that what you can give as an actor is important. You have to feel a great sense of responsibility about what you do. On a practical level what this means is that you have to promise not to miss work, not to miss class.

We have made a commitment to each other. You have to feel that there is a moral quality to that commitment. You have to understand that there was a time when a handshake reflected a moral commitment, that men would rather die than break a promise or betray what was implied in a handshake.

The actor has the ability to convey moral force, to help people understand that even a handshake has a moral significance. There is no limit to what an actor can make an audience feel and understand.

Writers are important. So are scenic artists and directors. But you have let them take over. We actors have to reclaim first place. That's what this class is really about.

THE WORLD OF THE STAGE ISN'T YOUR WORLD

The first thing you must learn to become an actor is what the theatre can mean. And how much it can mean. I'm not referring to the debased idea of the theatre as it exists today, but the theatre as it has existed for over 2,000 years.

A civilization isn't defined by how much money somebody made or how many BMWs people have in their garages. If you visit the Metropolitan Museum of Art, you won't see exhibits of people's bank accounts. The currency of civilization is Art. That's what's preserved in our museums and libraries.

You have the possibility of carrying these riches of two millennia inside you. But you cannot transmit what you have not received. So you must study theatre the way a priest or a rabbi studies scripture. You have the privilege of forging our link from that history to the future.

If the theatre today is debased, it's because *we* are debased. If we look around at America we see a place where people steal for a nickel, where people kill without a deep sense of guilt, where people have no respect for religion, where people dress carelessly, where people don't respect their bodies.

Inevitably the theatre must reflect all that. The word theatre comes from the Greek. It means the seeing place. It is the place people come to see the truth about life and the social situation. The theatre is a spiritual and social X-ray of its time. The stage can no more lie about who we are than an X-ray can. The theatre was created to tell people the truth about life and the social situation.

Two thousand years ago Sophocles wrote a play about a man named Oedipus, who killed a man and slept with his widow. The man he killed was his father and the woman he slept with was his mother. He had been warned that he would do this, but he thought he could outwit his destiny.

Oedipus did something in the social situation that was dangerous, something that threatened the entire social life of his community.

You still have some sense that certain behavior can be threatening to all our welfare. That was what Sophocles was writing about. He wanted to teach morality and justice.

We don't have to go back 2,000 years to understand this. In 1947 Arthur Miller wrote a play called *All My Sons* in which a father shortchanges the government in the airplane parts his factory manufactures. The result is that he may have been responsible for the death of his own son. His decision to place profits above responsibility means that all of us, every part of us is threatened.

Arthur Miller wants to teach morality and justice. So it was, so it is, and so it shall ever be. These are the subjects of theatre. If they aren't your subjects it's not too late to arrange for a tuition refund.

▼

You're here to prepare yourselves to ask big questions, to help great writers pose great questions. That's what writers have done from Sophocles onward. Part of your preparation must be to understand the language of the past and to make it compelling for audiences in the present.

You must be aware that even a subject of profound importance can be trivialized and degraded if you haven't the energy and interest to match it. We all know people who can be asking big questions but they might as well be asking you for a cigarette. If you're one of them now, you won't be for long.

Listen to yourselves. Listen to your neighbors. Are you hearing substance? Or have you become complacent with the dreary doggerel of everyday gossip? Here within these walls you will learn to raise any subject you discuss to its highest point.

One of the reasons I asked you to prepare something from Gibran is that his writing has a Biblical quality. It has size. Most of you, when you talk, are talking air. What you talk about rarely has any more interest or energy than if you were saying, "I need a cigarette."

You have to understand that the theatre is epic. It's large the way The Law is large, the way Family Life is large, the way growing trees are large — you must nurture them. You can't neglect them.

▼

Many years ago I went to Columbia University. I was interested in architecture. Specifically I was interested in how Carolingian architecture was transformed into Gothic. I was that kind of crazy student. I was already playing on Broadway, but I schlepped myself up to Columbia to study Carolingian architecture.

The teacher was Meyer Shapiro, one of the greatest critics of art and architecture. He allowed me into his classroom. I didn't think about paying, because I'm very abstract. Nobody asked me for money, so I just walked in at ten in the morning. (You're not so lucky in that respect. We always remember to ask you to pay.)

The other students in the class were graduate students. Do you know that the graduate students and myself didn't understand one word he said that first morning? Why? Because he couldn't get from Carolingian to Gothic without starting in the 6th Century B.C. From there he went into the Byzantine. And eventually we got to the Carolingian.

And, of course, everybody in the class said, "Yes, Mr. Shapiro. Of course, Mr. Shapiro." Then we read and studied all night at home in order to catch up with his world.

Sometimes I think my students feel the same. They're respectful. They say, "Yes, Miss Adler. Of course, Miss Adler." But what they're thinking is, "Get the hell on with this."

Well, you can't get the hell on with this. Either you get Meyer Shapiro doing Carolingian architecture. Or you will get The Show. And if I give you The Show I'm cheating you. If it's The Show you want, you don't want me. I'm not supposed to be the entertainment; you are. In Shakespeare's day thousands of people preferred bear baiting to *Hamlet*. If you're here to see bear baiting you've come to the wrong arena. Try the World Wrestling Federation. They're actors and bears both.

I'm giving you all of history in order to jumpstart your instrument, which is run down, to awaken your soul, which is in a state of catatonia.

Be honest. Do you read? If you don't read Dante or Keats or Dostoyevski, you don't. You don't discuss ideas. You don't know how to reach each other. You're skimming life.

Acting wasn't born today. It's a tradition of 2,000 years. In England to be considered great you have to play Hamlet or King Lear.

You don't have this tradition. You'll never be buried in Westminster Abbey. You're not going to be made a Commander of the British Empire or a member of the House of Lords. But you'll never really be great unless you aim high. *Death of a*

Salesman is as near as you will get to playing Hamlet. You have to be ready for *Death of a Salesman*. To play in the big plays your acting range, your stretch, your being, your lifeline has to be big.

You never are a great conductor unless you conduct the three B's, Bach, Beethoven and Brahms. You are never a great composer unless you write a symphony. You're never a great writer unless you write in the poetic style.

When *Time* magazine came to ask me about Marlon Brando, who was at one time my student, they said, "Is he a great actor?" I said, "We'll never know. He has greatness in him, but there is no actor in the world who knows whether he's great unless he plays the great parts."

▼

We have to restore theatre to its historical purpose, lift it to the level where it existed all over the world for thousands of years. To the point where we understand that what the playwright was saying was, These are the rules, these are the cosmic rules. That's what playwriting is about.

It's not easy to get from where we are today back to the place we once were. The skepticism of everyday life and the loss of artistic ideals creates an environment of irreverence. It seems more difficult for the contemporary student to discipline himself than it did in previous generations. Students frequently come to me smashed, physically and emotionally. Their relationship to life is completely deadened. Seemingly, they have no idea where they are or where they're going.

But there *is* a basic need in human beings that makes them want to expand themselves. There *is* a spark that wants to grow. That spark has to be kept alive. With a clear and hardworking effort, you can grow, you can graduate from callousness and emptiness into esthetic maturity. With proper training you can stretch your talents immeasurably. That's why we have the technique.

▼

The first aspect we work on is seeing, creating images for ourselves that energize what we say. When you say something, see what you're talking about. Don't open your mouth until you do.

That's why I want you to concentrate on seeing the differences between the different reds, the different blues — to see how you respond to them. An actor who has looked carefully at the red on the mailbox will never see it again without saying, "Ah, that's the red from my exercise." He will never look at the red of nail polish and confuse it with the red of the stoplight.

Acting is not an abstract activity. The actor must make everything he deals with real. If I have a chair onstage with me that chair must become the focus of my attention so that it's not just an abstract object. It's an object with which I have some relationship.

Sometimes a chair can help you define a play. When we see the father in Edward Albee's *The Death of Bessie Smith* we know almost everything we need to know about him because he's sitting on run-down wicker furniture on the porch. I must say there is nothing that says more who you are than run-down wicker furniture. There is something about it that says, "What happened to you? You used to be white and now you're chipped."

Albee's play is about a society that will allow a great artist to die just because she's black. The great Blues singer Bessie Smith died because a white hospital in the South would not admit her.

We never see Bessie Smith herself in the play, but Albee shows us a great deal about the culture that allowed her to die because of the color of her skin. The father sitting on the wicker furniture is a man full of hatred. He loathes his daughter, he loathes himself, he loathes black people, he loathes the mayor of the town, who will not see him. He represents the breakdown of the Southern order. But we can see it all in the run-down wicker furniture.

As for the chair in my hand, I know the precise shade of brown it is. I know every nick on its back. I know where the paint has come off. I know where the springs are pushing through the upholstery. I know if the legs are wobbly or if the arms need to be fixed.

I also know what the chair demands of me, whether it makes me sit up straight or whether it allows me to slouch. If I sit in a beach chair, how long does it take me to respond to the truth of where I am?

You will hear me say very often what Stanislavski said — truth in art is truth in circumstances, and the first circumstance, the circumstance that governs everything is, Where am I?

If I don't understand the chair completely, I'll be forced to fake it. That's the worst thing an actor can do. We have to take the same attitude toward a dramatic text. We have to understand it totally, have to know its every nick and eccentricity before we can feel comfortable with it. We have to understand what it demands of us. Otherwise we can't communicate it and we become fake. Is anything worse?

The actor knows how easy it is to lie, to fake. What he must do is surround himself with things that are true. As long as he can focus on those, he won't be tempted to lie.

▼

The actor is always in a specific circumstance. When you stand on stage to give us the ideas of Gibran. Ask yourself, "Where am I?" There are several ways to answer this question. You can be realistic. You can say, I am in the Stella Adler

Conservatory, on West 56th Street, in a room with white walls, with a platform with windows at the back. There are lights coming down on the platform.

Or you can be imaginative: "I am standing in a public square where people have come to hear me speak." If you are going to be imaginative, you have to be very specific. What kind of buildings surround the square? What part of the country are you in? What year? What time of year? What kind of people are listening to you? What are they wearing? What class are they? Is it an old square with historic buildings? Is it a park? If so, what kind of trees can you see? What kind of flowers? And so on, and so on, and so on. The more you concentrate on the circumstances that surround you, the more at ease you'll be.

Circumstances make us see. To be specific, we have to see where we're standing. We cannot see what isn't there. And nothing will be there until you put it in. If the actor sees it he can make his audience see it. That's the first rule of acting — there must be images.

The better the actor the more specifically he creates the circumstances. He always has a partner. Sometimes the partner is another actor on stage, with whom he communicates.

Sometimes the partner is the audience. When you stand on stage today to give us the ideas of Gibran, your partner will be the audience. Not just this audience of your fellow students, who are your friends and who will make every effort to encourage you and smile as if they understand what you're talking about, whether they do or not.

You must imagine the kind of audience you will have in a theatre, where no one knows you, where there will be little old ladies in the balcony who will have trouble hearing you. When you stand on stage it is imperative that those little old ladies hear every word you say and understand them. That's your job.

When you speak to somebody, whether it's another actor on stage or that little old lady in the balcony, the most important thing is to make them *see*. Communication is making someone

THE ART OF ACTING   37

else see what you see. If I talk about large trees with beautiful, large, yellow lemons, do you see them? You can't help but see them. Everything you say from the stage must be as visibly clear as that.

▼

I assign the popular essays in Gibran's *The Prophet* because they are concerned with the universal truths of marriage, children, giving, time and joy and sorrow. If you study pieces written only in the vernacular, by their nature they don't readily move from your head to your heart. The essay should open up your relationship to an idea, for the actor must be personally involved with the author's idea. It should carry the actor's interpretation.

Now when you've absorbed and learned some of Gibran's ideas, first you must make sure they're simple and clear enough that everybody — no matter how ignorant they are — understands what you're saying. The theatre is not just for smart people.

Your job is not to show us how clever and sophisticated you are, how you can use literary words. You have to understand his ideas as clearly and completely as if they were your own. And they have to matter to you as much as if they were your own for you to feel the importance of communicating them to others. I must feel the urgency of what you have to say. The need you feel to make the audience actually see what you've seen will push your voice forward.

Get used to the idea that you're not doing it as a student. You're doing it as an actor. If you were just a student you could do it in your dull street voice, looking at your feet. But as with everything you do on stage, now you must make it vital.

You become important as the idea enters into you. It's best not to pronounce the idea but rather to convey it so it's understandable to the audience. For that, the most serviceable vocabulary is the one close to what you do and who you are.

The essay should open up your relationship to an idea. Gibran, for example, says, "When you meet your friend on the roadside or in the marketplace let the voice within your voice speak to the ear of his ear for his soul will keep the truth of your heart as the taste of the wine is remembered when the color is forgotten and the vessel is no more." How can we communicate that simply and directly? Here is one way: When you speak to a friend say only what really matters to you, and he won't forget it.

After you have explained the idea, give your response to it. The essay has opened up your relationship to an idea, which is what we aim for.

You also must make us understand that these ideas are universal. If Gibran talks about pain we have to sense the pain he's describing is not someplace over there in another time. That pain is in you now. And it's not just a minor headache. It's a migraine.

It may be the pain of Vietnam or the pain of Bangladesh. It might be the pain of someone's death. It is a pain that's manifested itself in man for millions of years that throbs inside you.

Now I don't expect you to be able to do this just like that. You will fail. That's great. Here's a secret for you — that's the only way you can learn. Learning has to cost you something. If you fail but learn something from your failure, you will grow. I've been talking over and over again about size. You don't achieve stature unless you fail. You will only fail to learn if you do not learn from failing. Falling flat on your face will uplift you!

I would be very happy if in six months you came to me and said, "Miss Adler, I want to do the Gibran exercise again. Now I really understand what it was about." The fact that we start with Gibran doesn't mean it's trivial or that the exercise is easy. Far from it. It has the seeds of everything else we'll study.

Who would like to be first?

All right, Robert, that's very brave.

ROBERT: Gibran says of marriage . . .

STELLA: It's very nice of you to give the author credit, but when you stand on stage you represent him. When you say, "To be or not to be," you don't preface it by telling us, "Shakespeare says, 'To be or not to be.'" You just say the line. Do the same with Gibran.

ROBERT: Marriage binds two people forever but there should be spaces in their togetherness.

STELLA: That was clear, but let's have more of you. I need to have your reaction to his concept of the relationship. You have a lot of questions to answer in paraphrasing what he says. When marriage is entered into, do you think that it should be automatically forever? Do you approve Gibran's idea that marriage partners should not interfere with each other's personal freedom? Every major idea begs for a reaction, an interpretation.

Who wants to be next? Thank you, Jennifer.

JENNIFER: Time is the most precious thing we have. Before I read Gibran's essay I was constantly looking at my watch and wasting my time that way. After reading the essay, I learned to enjoy time.

STELLA: Very good, Jennifer, but what do you really mean when you say you enjoy time?

JENNIFER: Well, I appreciate things more when I am on my way somewhere. I don't rush the cab driver. I no longer rush the reading. I live for today and I live it more fully.

STELLA: Very good, darling. Jennifer has taken what

Gibran wrote and reacted to the idea. This is what we should do with the ideas of the playwrights — our job is to experience and interpret them. Gibran's essay opened up Jennifer's relationship to an idea, which is what is needed on the stage.

Ultimately we do not want the author himself on the stage. We need you, the actor, plus the author, so that the idea filters through the living performance.

▼

Do you see that all that is required of you, all that these exercises are about is to give you growth? You've got to grow up in order to be an actor. You've got to be a man to play John Gabriel Borkman or Richard III. You've got to be a man that knows a lot. However you cannot play Hedda Tesman or Shaw's Joan of Arc if all you know comes from the suburbs.

You can't go on stage unless you're filled with things that give you life all day long — and problems all day long! That's what develops you.

For the next lesson I want you to bring in an object from nature. Study it in such detail that you can stand on the stage and give it to us. If it's a flower, I want you to be able to distinguish between the shade of yellow at the very center and the shade of yellow around the edge of the leaves.

I also want you to bring back one of the reds or blues or whites you brought in this week and describe it in circumstances, that is to say, within its context.

If it was a blue on a lampshade, I want you to make us see the lampshade, which was made of plastic in the shape of an overturned soup bowl. The shade was on a wooden cylinder about three inches thick and a foot high. The wood was unfinished. So was the circular base. The lamp was standing on a table of gray formica. Next to the lamp is a photograph in a lucite frame. Get the idea?

I want you to give us these objects so we understand that this color and this object stand in a very specific time. If the lamp is plastic it can only be of our time. If the table is formica it can only be of our time.

If the lampshade is of silk, it could be of our time — but probably in a very wealthy household. If the table is mahogany it could be in our time — but either in a very old-fashioned household or a household furnished exclusively in antiques or one so poor it can only afford second-hand furniture.

When you act you need to create a world of a very specific time around you. The only way you can do that is to see your own world more clearly than you do.

I also want you to bring in some action that you observe in everyday life and make us see that we think it's ordinary but that it really isn't.

▼

You are in a profession of recognizing life as important and not casual. Thornton Wilder was a genius of understanding this. *Our Town* is all about really seeing what we've all taken for granted. In the last act Emily has died. She watches her own funeral and then she has a chance to go back and relive a day in her life. She is urged not to, but she insists. She decides she'll choose a happy day. Her wise mother-in-law tells her it's better to choose an unimportant day. "It will be important enough," Mother Gibbs tells Emily.

She selects her twelfth birthday. Everything that happens could not be more ordinary — a mother is yelling at her children to come down for breakfast. It happens all over the world and it always has. In the midst of the ordinariness, Emily (who, because she's dead, is not just participating in the day but also observing it) begs her mother, "Oh, Mama, just look at me one moment as if you really saw me."

What happens could not be more trivial, but Emily breaks away and says to the stage manager, "So all that was going on and we never noticed."

Finally Emily can no longer bear the intensity of what she's seeing. She asks the stage manager, "Do any human beings ever realize life while they live it? — every, every minute."

At first the stage manager answers, "No," then he adds, "The saints and poets, maybe — they do some."

We have accepted what's around us as just there. We accept it. We don't understand that what's around us has gone on for hundreds and hundreds of years, changing so slowly we don't see it happen. Therefore we lose the sense of ourselves and where we come from. We lose a sense of the continuity of history — and the sense that history continues in everyday life. You are living or re-living history every moment of your life.

You see a man going out to buy a paper. How many years have men gone to buy the paper? A couple of hundred years? And it's been happening all over the world. Buying a paper is not just something you see. It's something that existed before you saw it. And it has a history. An awareness of history will help you stop taking life and its activities for granted.

You see a man walking with his dog. He may be a young man or a man of 60 or 70. That has been going on for hundreds of years. He's talking to his dog in a special kind of voice. That too has been going on for hundreds of years. You see a man holding hands with a girl. How long has that been going on? Adam and Eve. It is *not* ordinary. Though you may be tempted to think it's ordinary, it's up to the actor to see how it's different.

You see a woman carrying food. What you don't see is that people have had to carry food from the beginning of time. What is historic is that today the woman carries food in a plastic bag from the supermarket. She doesn't have to carry vegetables from the field in a sack she wove herself.

You must recognize the significance of living every moment. You don't have to amplify it — just recognize it. Recognize history. Recognize you're a continuation of history.

It would be wonderful if you lived your life that way, but we all know that's not the case. That's why you need these exercises.

ACTING IS DOING

Acting and doing are the same. When you're acting you're *doing* something, but you have to learn not to *do* it differently when you *act* it.

We're going to spend a lot of time studying actions. For your first actions I'm going to ask you to do some terribly simple things, things impossible for you to fake. Eventually you must do everything on stage — no matter how complicated it is — as simply and directly as you do these things.

First look at the blackboard. Look at the piano. Look at the steps. Look at the doors. Look at me. Look at my vest. All right, now let's do that again. Look at the blackboard, the piano, the steps, the doors, at me, at my vest.

Nothing complicated. No question of what the action is or what it demands.

Now let's go a little further. Find the largest chair on the stage. Find the largest piece of furniture in the auditorium. Find the lights that aren't working. Find the people wearing glasses.

In each case I told you to do something and you did it. These are baby actions, little, miserable things. They were all doable. And that is what we have to learn in every action — to make it doable.

Notice I never said, "Find!" I never said, "Look!" I never

said, "Count!" I always said, "Count the *lights*, count the *chairs*, count the *number* of *eyeglasses*." I always said, "Find something, look at *some*thing." Always *some*thing specific. Acting is not a theoretical science.

An action has to go somewhere. It has to have an end. It can't just hang. Now if I said to you, "Count," it wouldn't work, would it? But if I say, "Count the blue blouses in the room," it works immediately. Every action has an end, an object. An action is weak unless you finish it.

▼

Now I want each of you to take a partner. Find the softest piece of clothing your partner is wearing. Now find the smallest lights that shine in your partner's pupil. Is that harder? Yes. What makes it harder? The end makes it harder. That's clear. So the end gives you the strength of action, defines the action.

If I ask you to find the largest vein on your wrist, it's harder. If I ask you to count the number of colors on the package, it's harder. The action is made hard or easy by the end.

In the last class I asked you to bring in an object from nature. What is the action? The action is to describe an object from nature. It is always useful to study nature, because nature is large and timeless. Most of the time we take it for granted. In doing so we demean life.

Sometimes, when a husband and a wife go on a trip together, he might say, "My God! Do you know what that is? Why, that's Notre Dame!" And she replies, "Yes, I know. I can see it." They are seeing in Notre Dame something entirely different. As actors you must make everything you see come alive.

Let us say it is a stone: "I saw a great big stone, a beautiful stone. It was gray and its surface was uneven. Around it there was grass, but patches of the grass were dead and had turned yellow." Is there anyone who did not see the stone or who could not reproduce what I said. It has to be that simple and that direct.

How hard or easy it is to describe what you brought in depends on the object you have selected. You'll hand it to me, then you'll go up on the stage and describe it, and I'll ask you some questions about it.

Who wants to go first? All right, Sheryl. As you can all see, Sheryl has brought in a lemon.

STELLA: What can you say about its shape?

SHERYL: It's like a tiny yellow football, but it has a little bump on each end.

STELLA: Good, Sheryl. What can you say about its surface texture?

SHERYL: It looks smooth, but the surface is actually covered with little dots. It's yellow, but it's not uniformly yellow. The little dots are slightly darker than the area between them.

STELLA: Very good, Sheryl.

Did you all see the lemon? Even if I were not holding it would you all be able to describe it to someone in another room?

Was there anything difficult about that? No. Sheryl used words we all understand. Don't use fancy words. Fancy words lead to fancy feelings. Don't use words like "circumvent" when you mean "get around." When you ask the butcher for two pounds of beef, he doesn't say, "Shall I circumvent the fat?" Actors are much more in the butcher business than in the academic world of the classroom and library. Tell me words that I fall in love with. "Circumvent" seems pretentious to me. Use words that reach me. Don't use words that fail to connect.

Who wants to be next? All right, Linda. Linda has brought in a rose.

LINDA: The rose is scarlet.

STELLA: Yes?

LINDA: It's about four inches in diameter.

STELLA: This isn't a math class. We don't want abstractions. We want to be able to see. Is it all scarlet?

LINDA: No. The edges are pink.

STELLA: What about the stem?

LINDA: The stem is a dark green.

STELLA: And?

LINDA: It's just green.

STELLA: Is that all that matters about the stem? What's the most obvious thing about the stem?

LINDA: I'm not sure.

STELLA: It has thorns! That's the most obvious thing about the stem of a rose! Sometimes it's harder to notice the most obvious thing than the little subtle things, but we must see everything. What else can you say about this rose?

LINDA: It's beautiful.

STELLA: That's too obvious. Look at the rose again. Do you see that it's curled up in the center where the pollen lay? Do you see how soft it is? Those are simple observations, but if you tell your partner that he'll certainly remember it. He'll certainly see it.

It requires a certain energy to make your partner see what you see and understand what you understand. Simply for you yourself to see and understand it is not enough. When you give me your rose, that is your play. You imagine your rose and you give it back.

The words are only the result of what you have seen. To give words alone is ridiculous. The words come only after seeing. That's why it never helps to study the words or to memorize. You risk killing the ideas and the objects you're dealing with.

▼

As actors, you must learn to like what you are talking about. For your images go to nature, to the real world, to such things as the sea, the sky, flowers. Don't go to the movies or TV — to a second form or a second-rate truth. Take things from life — food, animals, clothes.

I once was on a train to Pisa. Out of the train window you could see the town itself. To be able to look out of a train window and see the Tower of Pisa was an extraordinary sensation. A man sitting beside me had a travel folder in his hands. Instead of looking out the window, he preferred to study the pictures of the town in that folder. Of course he was an American.

One must go to nature for images that live. Don't take mechanical objects to describe. Don't take light bulbs or radios or dishwashers. They are cold and small. Nature is large and timeless. Go to the things that are forever, like a stone or a flower. The stone was there before you were born. It is there for you to see now and it will be there after you die. The stone has a certain size that makes it worthy of description.

As actors, you must realize that what you see is a miracle simply because it exists. After all, you chose this profession because other ways of life seemed impossible to you. In acting you would be more alive. Therefore, make those things you see around you live so that you can give them back from the stage.

What did you see that was beautiful? You must make me see it. Are you excited by it? You must work on your description until you can convey to me your inner excitement. "I saw the richest, deepest red carnation in the whole world." The carnation has to be in you and you cannot push the inner truth of that carnation. You must experience it before I can experience it.

You must give us the excitement of your choice. Don't explain it. Take us there. Show us something that belongs to you, then give it away.

The description is less important than the feelings that come out of the words. The excitement lies in your choice, your choice of animal, of flower, of food. Don't be cool in your descriptions. (If you're too cool you'll wind up not as an actor but as the manager of the company.) Don't be afraid of agitating your description by surrounding the object with details. But don't explain. One should not use too many words, and only those one likes. The feeling evoked by the description is more important than the description itself.

▼

Here's an exercise we can do together. Let's look at the sky. Take your time. Do you see it? What color is it? Is it blue? Blue mixed with what? Is it all the same shade of blue? Is the shade different closer to the buildings across the street than it is up higher? What shape are the clouds? Not the scientific name for the clouds. What shape do you say they are? Do you see that you could spend the rest of the class looking at the clouds and trying to describe them?

Do you see that if we'd looked at the sky two hours ago it would have been entirely different? And that if we look at it two hours from now it will be something else?

Every action takes place in a world. When I asked you to describe the reds, whites and blues in extended circumstances, it was a way of placing them in their world. Every time we perform an action we have to be aware of the world in which the action takes place. The more carefully we can see that world, the easier it will be to perform the action.

Who understands when I say that when you're on stage the props speak to you? They make it easier for you to do your job. But you have to see them. You have to listen to them. When you see a thing, it exists and has a life. See that life. Respect everything. Everything will speak back to you.

The next step is to see as clearly in your imagination as you do in life. When you work creatively with your imagination there is no higher form. It will open up in you what has been closed for years.

Your imagination consists of your ability to recall things you've never thought of. In order to do this readily, you must comprehend how rich your memory is. You have a bank account that you know nothing about, for the memory of Man is such that he forgets nothing he has ever seen, or heard, or read about or touched.

You use a tiny fraction of what you know. You know everything. It is all there. All you have to do is recall it. An enormous wealth of material therefore exists in the mind of the actor, never to be tapped except in plays. There is not a single thing that you've ever seen or heard or touched from the time before you were born that hasn't been stored within you.

If you confine yourself to the beat of your generation only, if you're bound within the limits of your street corner, alienated from every object or period that does not contain your own pulse, then you dismiss the world in general, you make everything foreign.

American actors greatly underestimate their wealth of human, or national, memory. In this area, they are the very opposite of their British co-professionals, who feel they stand for England itself. The typical British actor, when playing a Shakespearean king, believes he's portraying a not-so-distant relative. You have no relatives. You have dropped all tradition and sense of history, and that is harming you as actors.

To begin to exercise your imagination, you have to place a greater value on your store of knowledge and practice a higher personal appreciation of the self.

Acting is in everything but the words. Reporting on what you have seen and experiencing the seeing of it are two different things. One is for the newspaper and the other is for the stage. You can say, "She beat her baby," and that's reporting. Or you can say, "Look at her beat the baby. Isn't it terrible," and that is still too cool for the stage. One has to put it in the present, placing you there. You particularize: "Oh, my God, the baby, the baby. . ." And there you are at the place, in the present moment, and we in the audience experience what you see.

Consider the difference between "That poor horse is being whipped," and "Look, he's being whipped, that poor horse. It's horrible . . ." You have agitated the present so that we can actually experience what you have seen. The difference is between seeing it today and saying tomorrow that you saw it. A child is hit by a car. First comes the scream, then the experience.

What you see or experience now is different from what you recollect from the past. If a doctor is about to stick a needle into your vein to take a blood sample, you say, "Oh, I don't want that needle in me. It's horrible." You have experienced the pain of the needle first. Then you go home and explain what happened to your mother: "He stuck a needle into me, and it was horrible." The second, obviously, is more passive. It does not have the immediacy or impact of the first. The second is remembering life. The first, facing it.

The actor, however, can err on the side of overreacting in such situations. If I say to a student, here is a very long needle and the doctor is about to inject it into your arm, the student may be too ready with a reaction. This results from taking the reaction from within rather than from imagining the needle, from creating a response instead of actually feeling one.

The reaction cannot be forced. It has to be born. Holding out an imaginary bowl, I can say to a student, "This is very hot water. Give me your hand." The student will shrink back instantly. You have to say to yourself, I will not make *believe* it will happen. If I am properly receptive, it *will* happen.

I hope you see that being an actor is not just a job that begins when you arrive at the theatre in the evening. It's something for which you are constantly preparing.

▼

Now I didn't have a so-called normal childhood, because I lived with the greatest actor I've ever seen, who happened to be my father. Jacob P. Adler was recognized in America as one of the greatest actors of all time. When Stanislavski came to America he sought out my father because my father had played a role in Yiddish that Stanislavski was going to play in Russian and he wanted to know how my father had done certain things.

My father didn't give me a moment's peace. If we were walking in the street, he'd point to someone and say, "Look at her. Look at the way she walks. Look at him. Watch the way he uses his hands. Imitate her voice."

I was always being told to do something. I wasn't told just to walk. My father's eyes never stopped. All of his kids had to imitate everything. He didn't care whether we slept or not. At night we would be taken out of bed. Company would be there. "Get up and imitate your teacher," he would order us. We were acting all the time.

"Observe! Observe! Observe!" he'd tell us.

I was sitting in a box in the theatre with him once, and he saw a girl in the next box who had a nervous habit. He studied her and he started imitating her.

He never stopped for a minute. That's the way you become an actor. You cannot afford to confine your studies to the classroom. The universe and all of history is your classroom.

CLASS FOUR

THE ACTOR NEEDS TO BE STRONG

L ast time we began working on actions. Everything we do in the theatre is an action. That's what acting means. So there's nothing more important we can learn.

On the one hand acting is very simple. It's just *doing* something — and doing it as truthfully as possible. What makes it more complicated is that we're doing these actions on the stage, and we must always be worthy of that platform.

That platform, that goddamn platform, holds you up. It gives everything you do a weight, an importance. If I walk around down here, I'm just walking around. If I walk on the stage, on that platform, everyone who watches knows my walking must have some meaning, some significance.

One of the first questions you must ask yourself is, How do you want to be seen on that platform? Would you like to be seen at your best? When you speak, would you like to speak your best?

▼

For the acting life you can't bring in a broken body. This is something I'm afraid your society can't teach you. You live in a society where it's common to see people with broken bodies, bodies that turn inward, bodies that turn downward.

Do you see anybody slouching in Greek sculpture or on Greek vases? No, the bodies go upward. They didn't let you act unless you knew that. They didn't let you play anything because they knew and the English know and the French know and the Germans know — the only people that don't know are the Americans. Man will definitely be broken if he goes inward.

Horses have it. Dogs have it. Certain cultures have it and certain cultures don't. The spine reaches up and the head sits there. Everything is comfortable. You must always be conscious of aspiring upward. Even if you sit down you don't *go* down. If you think the whole body goes down when you sit you're revealing something about your character.

You have no society to show you. Your fathers have been broken, and some of your grandfathers already were broken. How many people have been allowed to walk badly? Has anybody made you understand anything about this? I want you to be committed to the idea that your body must pull you up.

The same is true of your voice. For the stage you can't have a voice that turns inward, a voice that mumbles. It's better to have a voice that's too big than one too small. If it's too big you can always modify it.

Most of you can make your butcher understand when you say, "Give me another piece of steak," but that won't carry you when you get on that platform. Any actor can talk on television, but few television actors can get up on stage. The stage kills them. You have to stretch your instrument so that even if you whisper, "Hey, hey, come over here," it carries to the back of the room.

Your voice needs to stretch. You need to find your tone to make yourself understood. You must have an acting voice. I don't care how horrible it sounds, but I must have volume.

Unless you can talk, you can't act. You are dull. And you have to be told that.

A good exercise, one that's easy to do and will help you build your voice, is to read an editorial aloud every day. First, read it in your normal voice, and your "normal" voice should be getting bigger and bigger, stronger and stronger. Next, read it as if you want someone 15 feet away from you to hear and understand it. Read it as if the audience were across the table, then across the room, then across the street — 50 feet away. Add space as your vocal muscles warm up and strengthen.

Talking goes *out*, doesn't it? You cannot talk *in*. Only demented people talk inward. You talk to be heard, to be understood. What does your hand do when you say, "Hello?" What do you do? You go *out*. Whenever you talk, you reach out. OUT. OUT. It's a madness to talk in. It makes no sense.

Why? Because everything has its nature. Every time we analyze an action, we have to try to understand its nature or purpose. The nature of talking is . . . OUT. The nature of walking is . . . solid.

The nature of the body — what is the nature of the body? Think of a child. In a baby the feet push, the hands reach. Always striving up.

If you haven't got that nature, you have to fix it. It's not so good to talk in. And it's not good for the body to go in. What if a tree grew in? Would you like that?

When your body is always pulling you upward and when your voice is strong enough to fill the room, you'll be worthy of standing on the stage. For now, I just want you to feel comfortable on this platform where you hope to make your life.

I want you to get up and stand on it. It holds you, yes? Now remember that it's there for you. And you don't need to draw away from it. Sometimes actors aren't sure they have the courage to stand here. Sweet, sensitive actors — sometimes they're not sure they can stand on their own two feet. But this platform is always here. Does the earth hold you up? Is it always going to be there? The same is true of this platform.

Now walk on the stage. Walk around. Does it hold you?

What is your action? I'm always going to be asking you, What is your action? The answer here and now is simply to walk around the stage.

It's different from a walk around the park. It's different from a walk around an airplane. It's not a very interesting action, but it has its own nature. Walk up and down. Walk to your seat and back again. That's the most you have to do in this action.

An action is something you always give yourself and is something you can do. You define the object of your action, and you make it something you can handle. This is very basic. Stanislavski doesn't have to help you with this problem. Mr. Harold Clurman doesn't have to help you with this problem. Even the Actors Studio doesn't have to help you. Defining an action you can perform is something well within your capability.

What makes it complicated? When you walk on the street you may or may not be aware of the world around you. When you're on stage, is there a world around you? There is always a world around you. But on stage, very often, you have to create that world. If you walk around without a world, it makes your action self-conscious. You must always fill the stage with your imagination. Surround yourself with it.

▼

Let's begin with a very simple action, something you've just done, coming into class. Maybe you remember how you came into class today, maybe you don't. It's not a question of reproducing exactly what you're just done. We're not here to be so literal-minded. Acting is not just imitating everyday behavior. It's capturing the essence of it. It's giving the audience the idea of an action. What happens on the stage must be more precise, more intense, more interesting than everyday behavior.

As you do this exercise you must project to an audience that you're coming into an acting class. Coming into class is not the same as coming into a funeral parlor or even coming into a theatre.

Now gather up your things, go outside and come back in.

Hurry up! Hurry up! How much thought does this take?

All right, let's examine what you did. Linda, you borrowed paper from Jennifer as you came in. That was good. It's not good enough to come in *with* something. It's much better to start doing something outside and finish it when you get inside. Objects are not enough. You must not just *have* something. You must *do* something.

Robert, you were putting on a jacket. I know what that was about. You were thinking, "She doesn't like men *not* to have jackets." But the audience doesn't know that. So even though it's based on a clear perception, it's not one that will register with the audience.

Jeremy, you tucked in your shirt. That isn't truthful. It has no justification. You don't walk around with your shirt sticking out. So you had no need to do it.

To take out a pencil is not enough of an action. Most of you, to show you're in the theatre, are looking through a script. You give the impression that you're reading. That was vague. None of you came in actually reading at the start of class.

If we gave the idea that you were searching for something in a script, however, actively searching, that would be valid.

You don't show "coming into class" by bringing in coffee, even if that's how many of you actually came in earlier. Class is not about eating and drinking. You're giving the audience false impressions. They'll think you're going to a baseball game.

Too many of your ideas come from the street. You're not going to a rehearsal for a television show.

Even for something as simple as coming into a room, coming into a specific room, there must be preparation. We, the audience, have to have a sense of the place where you come *from* and the place you've come *to*. How are the circumstances of each different? We have to have a sense of you doing something, not just wandering aimlessly. Preparation saves you the humiliation, the degradation, the loneliness, the panic of coming on the stage empty-handed.

▼

The stage will always support you. It will never leave you. You can die on it, and it won't leave you. When you die, it surrounds you. That's even better. But you must always be worthy of standing on it, of receiving the stature it will confer on you.

Every time you get on the stage you must take it seriously. You must think out what you do. Getting on stage is never something casual. You project something to the audience by what you wear, but it's more important to project something by what you do. The audience will be reading you regardless — you can't project nothing, only the right thing or the wrong thing.

If you're playing a doctor coming in to examine a patient, you can convey that to the audience by wearing a stethoscope. But that's static. We have to see you in action, studying the patient's chart, for example. A good playwright doesn't start his play with words. He starts with a place, and the actor has to give the audience, immediately, a clear sense of that place. Every time an actor has to speak, he must ask himself, What is there that *makes* me speak? All this requires preparation.

At one time in my classes every student's home was stripped for what the play needed. If you needed a lace tablecloth, you brought one from home or you borrowed one from a friend. One student brought in real candelabra. You would bring all these things from home so you could start from something truthful. Your home would be empty but the set would be truthful.

I'm afraid that you don't know where you are. You don't know your stage. And as long as you don't know where you are, you cannot act. Only in an insane asylum do people not know where they are. Even if you are playing a lunatic in an asylum, you the actor must still know where *you* are.

You must be familiar with every place that's given to you. You have to be able to say, "I am at home here." That comes before anything, before words, before talent!

Stanislavski says about the great Italian actor Salvini that when he played Othello he'd come to the theatre three hours before the curtain went up just to walk around the stage. Why did he do that? It was to immerse himself in the situation and circumstances.

Many of you have had teachers who said to you, "When you walk onstage, you open the door and then you close the door. Then you take an empty bottle and take a drink."

Well, tell those teachers they're liars. Stella Adler says they're liars.

Every action has its own preparations, its own requirements, its own demands. In order to pick up a bottle you have to say, How much does it take to lift the bottle? You have to work on it for at least twenty minutes. You have to lift the bottle when it's empty and lift the bottle when it's full. You have to do it until the muscles remember how much it takes.

Practice opening a jar. First do it when the top requires only normal strength to open. Then do it when the top is loose. Finally, practice opening a jar fastened too lightly. Practice it over and over until your muscles remember just how much strength and energy are required in each case.

Another useful exercise is threading a needle. First practice with a real thread and a real needle. Now just use the thread and react as if you're putting it into the needle. Now just use the needle and react as if you're putting the thread into it.

Next take the needle and thread and sew an imaginary hem

on a small piece of material. Do it over and over again so that you can eventually do it with two objects but not the third, the needle and the piece of material, but not the thread, the needle and thread, but not the material.

This has nothing to do with the mind. You have to respect the muscles. You're able to work because the muscles work. The muscles aren't like the mind. The mind is very complicated. The muscles aren't. Once you get them used to an activity, they remember it.

But the muscles don't accept lies. The muscles are very precise. They can tell the difference between a full bottle and a half-full bottle, between a jar whose lid is loose and one whose lid is much too tight.

Every prop you use on stage should represent a challenge. They're all foreign. You must work with them until you make them your own.

Every prop you use has got to pass through your imagination. Don't just take something from the stage manager. He doesn't care how good you are. He's just rounded up a bunch of objects. You have to make these objects yours. Realism means the ability to be at home on stage, and the way you do that is to make every object around you meaningful. You do that through the imagination.

Ninety-nine percent of what you see and use on the stage comes from imagination. On stage you will never have your own name and personality or be in your own house. Every person you talk to will have been written imaginatively by the playwright. Every situation you find yourself in will be an imaginary one. Every word, every action must be filtered through the imagination.

Write this down, "*Until a fact passes through your imagination, it is a lie.*"

The imagination works very fast. An actor must see fast, not slowly, think fast, and imagine fast. In class, in exercises to stimulate the imagination, I look for instantaneous reactions from the students. For the imagination to come quickly, all the actor has to do is let go. This is an exercise you should do often.

▼

The principle of seeing is to take in an image carefully, to experience what you take in and let it grow. You must see something in your head vividly and accurately before you can describe it. Only then can you give it back and make your partner or the audience experience what you have seen.

Therefore, understand the significance of keeping your eyes open and taking everything in visually. Life feeds you reality. Plays feed you imaginatively. When you describe something, it must be born in you. The difference between reporting and faithfully, imaginatively representing it is what makes you an artist.

The most common, inartistic way of observation is something I call Banking. It deals only with cold facts and objects. If I ask someone, "What do you have there?" and he, holding a handful of bank notes, replies, "Five, ten, fifteen, twenty, thirty — yes, I have thirty dollars in cash." And if, describing what he saw at the grocery, he says, "I saw some grapes and pears and bananas," then he makes a good banker. But not a good actor. He sees things as an accountant.

You must allow the objects to speak to you, to register personally what you have seen. If the man with the bank notes says, "I have some bills here that are rather dirty. Perhaps we can get them changed." And if, referring to the fruit, he says, "I saw fantastic pears that were big but looked too expensive to buy. Then I saw those wonderful Malaga grapes, long and very sweet. They also had the baby ones, the little green ones — the ones you can eat by the pound, and they're very cheap." That's more the actor's way.

That's what preparation is about. When you've done your

preparation properly you know how to come into a room. You know how to use the stage. You know how to justify moving around the stage. You learn how to do it all truthfully.

You learn to justify, not just to pick up an empty bottle and "make believe" it's real. Don't do that to yourself. It's a bad habit. It's a lie, and your body will react to the lie. You can fool your mind very easily. You have to work much harder to fool your body. It understands a lie immediately.

The reality you create on the stage by opening a jar or threading a needle isn't so that the audience will believe in you. It's so that you'll believe in yourself. Acting is truthful when you yourself are convinced. That's one of the essences of realism, and it's accomplished by doing very ordinary things.

For next week practice these simple actions: clean imaginary mud off your shoe, take an imaginary feather off a real skirt or trousers. Pretend that there is glue on your hand, take one hand at a time, wash it and see that each finger is clean of imaginary glue. Learn the sensory truth of muscular memory.

DEVELOPING THE IMAGINATION

If you'd come here to study a musical instrument, one things you'd have to learn is the proper way to warm up. You'd practice so that before a recital you'd know you were in control of your fingers, of your breathing, that you were ready to get the most out of your instrument.

As actors, our instruments are our bodies, and so we have to keep them in optimum condition. If we were pianists, how could we do our work if the keyboard sagged? You must not sag. I cannot look out into the classroom and see a bunch of coats that have slipped off their hangers.

I have told you actors should not easily get sick. Nor should they get tired. They belong to a different class of people. They don't give in. They hold themselves together, discipline themselves, take care of themselves. They're alert, bright and interesting. They don't succumb to middle-class-married fatigue.

The general laxity of the society we belong to, which promotes self-indulgence, is not good for theatre.

We have to have proper posture, which has a great effect on the way we breathe. We have to be in good physical condition. To work on the stage, we must possess enormous energy.

▼

There's a wonderful story about the great Italian actor Salvini. They asked him at the age of 70 to play the role of Romeo. To be Romeo you have to be very, very limber. Well, he said, he would like to do Romeo, but he required about seven months to limber up. Limbering up is not very interesting for an actor. But it's essential for us to do our job.

Salvini had to jump as Romeo. He had to stretch and practice, so the performance would be easy for him. You are not as old as Salvini, but you cannot be any less prepared. A body in good condition must be second nature to you.

Yet the most important thing we have to do is condition, to limber up the mind. Learn to stimulate the imagination. The imagination is what animates the instrument, keeps it in tune. It's the ignition key. Without it, nothing else works.

▼

We have worked on exercises to sharpen your ability to see, to distinguish between different shades of red and white and blue and to see how we react to the differences, to look at the world around us and see what makes it special, what makes it historic, to look at nature and see how rich it is, how stimulating it is to look at the same little bit of sky at different times of day and see how remarkably it changes.

But there is another kind of seeing that is equally important. There are a million things inside you that you have to learn to see.

Being an American has sapped your energy. It cuts off the feelings, the memories, the emotions, the instincts, the backgrounds. Why? Because we're "independent!" We imagine we can start over anytime we want. Isn't that absurd? You didn't even start fresh the day you were born. You were born into a pattern of life. You must begin entering into other people's lives,

to help you get beyond that boring, personal, egocentric quality you take for "real" life.

You have to get beyond your own precious inner experiences
now. I want you to be able to see and share what you see with an
audience, not just get wrapped up in yourself. Strasberg is dead.
The actor cannot afford to look only to his own life for all his
material nor pull strictly from his own experience to find his
acting choices and feelings. The ideas of the great playwrights
are almost always larger than the experiences of even the best
actors.

A great disservice was done to American actors when they
were persuaded that they had to experience *themselves* on the
stage instead of experiencing the play. Your experience is not the
same as Hamlet's — unless you too are a royal prince of
Denmark. The truth of the character isn't found in you but in
the circumstances of the royal position. The action of Hamlet,
to decide whether to live or die, has to match his circumstances,
not yours. Your past indecision on who to take to the prom
won't suffice.

Whatever the activity on the stage, you must first create the
circumstances. Stanislavski said you cannot have dinner on the
stage. What he meant is that you have to get away from the
abstract and into the particular. First you have a knife and fork.
Then you have a table with a lace tablecloth and simple silver
candlesticks. Then you have a plate with food and a soup spoon.
All these things are in the nature of the activity, which is having
dinner. The circumstances of the activity must be created before
anything else. By changing the circumstances, however, you can
change the mood of the scene.

If the tablecloth is not lace but some rough fabric, if there is
no tablecloth at all but a kerosene lamp, it will be a very different kind of dinner. The circumstances are dictated by the play,
and your imagination must be equal to the play's demands.

To begin to exercise your imagination, you have to place a
greater value on your store of knowledge. You're a storehouse of

images, not just the things you've seen, but the things you've imagined. Those images are very powerful. They will turn on your ignition. They will engage your body and mind.

From now on you must only live imaginatively. You will see and act in imaginative circumstances. To do this isn't hard if you accept that everything you can imagine has in it some truth for you. The actor's job is to de-fictionalize the fiction. If you need a lemon tree but have never seen one, you will create some kind of lemon tree for yourself, and the more details you give it, the more you'll accept that you've seen it.

You've imagined it. Therefore it exists. Most of acting lies in this minute knowledge of what you see and what you do. Anything that goes through your imagination has a right to live.

▼

Let's start with an easy exercise. You're walking along a country road. Know where you are. Look at the sky. Where is the sun? How long is your shadow? What is the road like? Is it bumpy? Does it distort your shadow? What kind of clouds are in the sky? What kind of birds do you see?

A fence lines the road, enclosing a meadow. How green is the grass? How tall is it? Are there cows grazing on it? If so, what color are they? Tell me three or four things that make the cows logical and real.

A long branch has fallen across the road. How recently did this happen? Is the foliage on it still green? Or is the branch long dead? How much effort does it take to pick it up and throw it into the field?

You see a dirt road that runs off to the right. Follow it. What kind of trees grow alongside it? Do they have fruit? Is it ripe?

The road leads to a wooden bridge. Does it look safe? What kind of railings does it have? It crosses a pond. What kind of fish can you see? Is the water too muddy to see fish? On the other side of the pond is a rope tied between two trees. Some clothes are hanging from the line — a child's pajamas, socks, a man's denim shirt, an old kitchen table cloth, overalls.

Look at the overalls. Notice their shape. How faded is the material? How often and at what spots have they been repaired? What pattern is on the tablecloth? How tall is the grass under the clothes line?

What you've seen is now entirely yours.

In a play the playwright is never going to give you a table-cloth that belongs to you. That is your job. His script will simply say, "tablecloth." You will have to determine how old it is, how wrinkled, how threadbare, how fresh, how starched. The playwright will only indicate what it is. You will have to make it come alive.

If the playwright indicates the day is fine, you will have to imagine a sky that is blue, with fleecy white clouds and birds flying in formation. The discovery of what is fine about it will be up to you. The playwright is never going to give you a country road that belongs to you. He will only say, "I was walking along a country road." You'll have to supply the details, saying to yourself, "It's dusty, the color of rust. There are corn fields on both sides."

As you work on the scene, the aliveness of it is what you act, not the facts. The facts will remain dead until you realize that each thing has life. As actors, you must give us the miracle of life, not the facts. For the spectator, you must give back life and not death.

▼

Life in the theatre isn't necessarily when you get money from performing. It isn't when you sign a contract. It isn't even when you are in a play. It's when you understand it. If you understand it, you'll know why you want to act, and if you don't understand it, you won't want to act.

You're painters. The palette comes from yourself. Underneath the words you paint with is you. If not, the words are empty. And don't constricted emotionally by taking the American Puritan ethic as your model. In England, the acting comes from the Elizabethan era, not the Victorian.

▼

Let's do another exercise. Let's imagine the robe of a Chinese emperor. One of our problems as Americans is our attitude is so practical, so no-nonsense that we reduce everything to our level. The imagination allows us to live in a larger, more beautiful, more exciting world.

First imagine the fabric for the emperor's robe. Is it fine quality linen? Is it silk? How heavy is it? Is it red? Is it gold? What shade? How long is it? Does it have to be supported by court attendants? How many? What is the pattern? How fine are the stitches? Is it something from nature? Is it the leaves of some tree? Is it the wings of a bird? A realistic bird? A fantasy bird? Is the pattern symmetric? Abstract?

There are no "correct" answers. And your objective in answering isn't to please me. It's to fire your own imagination, your own enthusiasm. And to communicate to the audience.

A student once said she was afraid of me — except when I smiled. I told her in that case I'd failed her. There are not many smiles in the theatre. If I gave her the impression there would be, I was preparing her for a career full of confusion and unhappiness. The person you have to please is yourself. But you'll go nowhere if you make it easy to please yourself. You have to be as demanding as you can.

All right, who would like to imagine for us the robe of a Chinese emperor. All right, Jennifer.

JENNIFER: "Mine is an orange brocade robe."

STELLA: I have to interrupt you, Jennifer. You're speaking like a little girl. (*imitating her*) "Mine is an orange brocade robe . . . Period." You've gone too fast. You're in too much of a hurry to reach the period. If I were describing the robe, I might say, "It was an orange robe, a very bright orange robe." You would have a sense of my seeing it and not being able to describe it immediately, searching for the proper words.

JENNIFER: I saw an orange brocade robe. It extended about two feet in back of the Emperor. It was embroidered in emeralds and diamonds all around the perimeter of it, and it had emeralds crisscrossed with rubies in the back, and it was filled with diamonds.

STELLA: It's much better, but it's still not right. It is studied, You are repeating sentences. I don't feel you're seeing it for the first time, seeing it clearly and precisely. You're giving me the emeralds and diamonds because you think that's what I want.

JENNIFER: (*after a long pause*) I see a long, beautiful, strange brocade robe. It's a very bright shade of orange. Around the edges are ermine, pink and white fur. It's sparkling, with studded diamonds arranged along the shoulders. In the back are even more sparkles and a row of emeralds, crisscrossed with a row of rubies . . . "

STELLA: This time you've really *seen* and she was really *talking*. Even the words you used were livelier and more natural. She improved on the description by extending it.

Did you notice that this time as Jennifer described the robe she began to giggle? That's significant. The first time she was simply reporting. Her last attempt was a piece of acting.

There's a big difference between a newspaper and the stage. The reporter must be objective, cool. The actor must be full of passion. If he's too cool he's better off as the manager of a company, not someone who appears on the stage.

We have been so deadened by television that we're like the surgeon who can slice open a body without feeling. He feels less than the anesthetized patients. In an operating room this is required. On a stage it kills the patient.

▼

We have a dilemma. We don't want what we see to be flat and without interest. But we don't want to overdo it so people think we're "pushing." The answer is that we must be truthful. The more details we imagine, the more honest and believable and energetic our responses will be. Nine tenths of your acting lies in the minute knowledge of what you see and what you do.

The actor is like a writer, full of impressions that speak to him. He does not say, "I'll have bacon and eggs." That's the way a clerk without a job speaks.

When the actor gets bacon and eggs he sees them on the plate, with some potatoes — the kind with bits of onion and green pepper. He sees the waitress. He sees the table and the restaurant, with all its rushed activity. He sees that the floor has dirt on it but the table is spotless. The coffee is weak, and the cup doesn't hold much, so he constantly has to catch the waitress's attention.

He looks around and sees that at all the tables no one is really paying any attention to each other. Everyone is in a hurry. Their gazes wander. Sometimes they look at the door to see who comes in.

The actor takes this all in. He isn't there just to eat, pay his check and leave. He *lives* there, watching, seeing, understanding. He asks himself, "What is this? What am I looking at?" — the way a writer or a painter does.

As actors, you must give us the miracle of life, not just facts.

Sergeant Joe Friday only wanted the facts. He's a cop. He wants to keep people calm. You want to stir them up.

One way we can enliven the imagination is to push it toward the illogical. We're not scientists. We don't always have to make the logical, reasonable leap.

Looking at a pair of glasses, I can let my imagination travel. I suppose a lot of people wear glasses, but they're really rather ugly, just two pieces of glass. They're not meant for anything but to see through. I used to wear glasses, but I've given them up. I guess I made the sacrifice because glass has no qualities in it. Wouldn't you feel much better if there were wine in this glass, or whiskey? But by itself, this piece of glass has no personality.

The rims of the glass are opaque. Do you know stones that are opaque? They are the colors of death, the pale greens. It's nice when they're amber, like amber earrings. Amber earrings change color. People don't wear amber any more, except in Paris, where the shops are filled with it. It is very hard for a Frenchman to give up anything.

If I were a psychiatrist I might call this free association, though I'd want it to be a lot more personal and introspective. In acting we call it "traveling." You choose some object and see where it takes you imaginatively. I see a red chair, and it takes me to Venice, and Venice reminds me of the shade of robe in a portrait of a cardinal by El Greco in the Metropolitan.

Looking at a silk flower takes me to Chinatown in San Francisco, to looking at antique clocks, to an acupuncturist's office, to listening to an artist singing after dinner, to the portraits of my parents.

In doing this exercise you become aware of what you didn't know you knew. It's like rummaging through a second-hand furniture shop. You never know what you'll come across or what you can use.

There are times when we can let the imagination roam. Other times we need to rein the imagination in.

▼

One of our exercises is describing cats. I want you to describe three cats: the Park Avenue cat, the Rego Park cat and the Ninth Avenue cat. Why do you suppose I ask you to do all three? It's to make you aware of differences in class. In America we pretend we're all equal, but we know better.

The Park Avenue cat is going to be a purebred, probably a Persian, with carefully groomed white fur and an imperious expression. She'll get dinner in her own little dish. Somewhere in the pantry will be her litter box, which a servant keeps impeccably clean.

She'll have a whole battery of pills to ensure her coat stays lustrous and sleek, vitamins to keep her in good health. She probably won't have claws, to preserve the Park Avenue furniture.

The biggest contrast will be the Ninth Avenue cat. Without claws, she'd be a goner. She has to defend herself against rats that might be as big as she is. She's also going to have to fend off dogs and other cats.

If she's lucky some storeowner might open a can of food and leave it on the sidewalk. Otherwise she has to pick through the garbage. Fortunately, on Ninth Avenue, there's tons of it.

She's obviously not going to be pure white if she lives on Ninth Avenue. She's probably going to be several colors and overall a little sooty. She's going to have clumps of fur because nobody brushes her. She's going to have scratches and maybe even clots of blood from the fights she's been in.

Her eyes, assuming she has both of them, are going to have a nervous quality, darting here and there. She hasn't the luxury of sitting still or grooming herself. She's responsible for her own survival, and it's not easy.

The Park Avenue cat is used to stillness and serenity. The

Ninth Avenue cat is used to noise all day — the taxis screeching by, the garbage men throwing sacks of garbage into the dumpsters with automatic lifts that carry them to the top with a loud, grinding sound.

The Rego Park cat is going to be somewhere in between. She won't be as pampered as the Park Avenue cat, and she may not be a purebred, but she's not as tough and wary as the Ninth Avenue cat. She may not have her own dish, like the Park Avenue cat, but she's not going to miss any meals.

She also may be able to go outside and do a little mousing. If so, she's got to have claws, and besides, the furniture she might harm isn't as precious. It may even have plastic slipcovers over it.

Do you see why an actor has to understand these differences and how the imagination helps him understand?

A student of mine once described an actor's room in a house outside Boston in the 1860's. She described the bed with its iron frame, the old coverlet on the bed, the quilt on the couch, the old-fashioned bureau and all the objects on it, the sort of paintings on the wall — all out of her imagination. Somewhere she drew out of herself all this material — a composite of what she knew and what she didn't know she knew.

One thing an actor cannot be is ignorant. An actor has to read. he has to know paintings and music, because they help him understand the past. They provide nourishment for his imagination.

Creating imaginatively is what acting is about. You don't need to say you don't know the room, that you cannot possibly have ever known it. You create the room, just as you create the robe, and it becomes yours. You must say to yourself, somehow I can make that robe work. It is, in fact, your job as an actor.

Eventually your imaginative reach will extend to other things, until you can say, I know how it feels to be in mourning, how it feels to be isolated, what it means to be abandoned, what it's like to be engaged or to be married.

Aspects of your imaginative powers will startle you.

▼

For the next class I want you to build three gardens: the garden of the French embassy in Washington, D.C., the garden of an Italian working class family in a Boston suburb, and a rundown yard in Mexico.

Use both what you know and what you imagine. Make them work hand in hand.

You'll come up on stage and give us a tour. You'll walk around showing upstage left a certain topiary in the French embassy garden or downstage right a trellis in the Italian garden or a cactus in the Mexican garden growing dead centerstage.

Over and over I find myself telling you, the truth in art is the truth in circumstances. "Where am I?" is the first question you must ask when you go on stage, before you perform any actions at all. Building the gardens is our first step in understanding how to feel at home on stage.

MAKING THE WORLD OF THE PLAY YOUR OWN

Actors feel uncomfortable in the wings. Even if they don't have full scale stage fright, they're nervous. That's not hard to understand. Actors have nothing to *do* in the wings. They don't belong there. Stagehands belong there. They have things to do there. We just wait there before we go on stage.

The only way we can make our waiting useful and not an occasion for unnecessary anxiety is to focus on what we will do when we go onstage. Once we get on stage the set designer and the lighting designer will give us help in understanding where we are. We'll have our fellow actors to work with. While we're backstage it's all in our hands.

We can examine our costumes and take cues from what the buttons tell us about the era our character lives in, or the class of the man who wears a suit with such buttons. Maybe a prop we're holding will help us enter into the world of the play.

There will be people who will tell you to use your time back-stage doing a certain kind of breathing or relaxation exercises. That's all right. You certainly don't want to go on stage with your body tense.

But the main ally we have in making that time useful is our

own imaginations, which is why we must develop them. I asked you to prepare three gardens. Every time you go out onto the stage you are, in effect, preparing a garden, a setting in which you feel comfortable. You have to build an imaginative relationship with the set, the props. They have to be as familiar to you as the furniture in your bedroom.

Who wants to take us through the garden of the French embassy in Washington, D.C.? All right, George.

GEORGE: When you drive up . . .

STELLA: I'm going to stop you. Driving up is irrelevant. We don't care about the parking lot.

GEORGE: A valet parks your car.

STELLA: All right, I'll accept that. That way we know we're dealing with something very formal. Go on, George.

GEORGE: You enter through high wrought iron gates. They have a graceful design — the ironwork has curves like plants but absolutely symmetrical, and in the middle you have, in very elegant carving that echoes the curves around them, the letters R and F, which stands for Republique Française.

STELLA: Very good, George.

GEORGE: As you walk in, you go along paths of pebbles.

STELLA: Good. You know, in the 19th century, when the wealthy had armies of servants, they had people who spent hours just raking the pebbles. Go on, George.

GEORGE: Along the paths you see hedges, and you know a staff of gardeners keeps them perfectly manicured. In the center of the garden you have a fountain that looks like it must have been imported from France in the middle of the 19th century. In the center is a goddess carved from black marble. It's Diana the huntress, and she is aiming her bow and arrow skyward. All along the rim are jets of water shooting at the statue, and the sun makes the wet marble gleam.

STELLA: Very good, George. Whatever you put into the embassy garden must be imposing. It must be elegant. It is there for effect, to impress whoever is lucky enough or important enough to be invited.

All right, who would like to do the garden of the working class Italian family in the Boston suburbs? All right, Natalie.

NATALIE: Right next to the house is a bed of pansies and daffodils.

STELLA: Remember, this is a working class family. Maybe they have pretty flowers, but there should be a sense that everything has a function. They're more likely to give that space over to vegetables — a row of tomatoes, maybe some arugala, some peppers, some lettuce, definitely some zucchini.

NATALIE: I was going to give them a little grape arbor.

STELLA: If you do, you should have a very clear idea of how grapes grow. In any case you should be able to stand on the stage and see everything clearly enough that you can show it to us. Maybe you'll have to crouch down to show us the first little sprouts of what was just planted a few weeks ago. The action of crouching will be dictated by what you see. Everything you do on stage should be dictated by the circumstances the character finds himself in.

In the Italian garden you're not trying to impress anybody. The only people who are invited here are friends and relatives. If there's going to be a statue in this garden, it's going to be the Madonna. If there's a table, it's going to be a picnic table. You have more work to do, Natalie.

Who would like to give us the yard of a Mexican house in a town near the Texas border? All right, Jason.

JASON: The house itself is a trailer. It's not very far from another trailer. So the yard is the space between them.

STELLA: Good, Jason.

JASON: The yard consists of sand rather than soil. All it can support is a little cactus. Near the cactus is a broken toy that belongs to one of the children who live there.

STELLA: Good, Jason. You may sit down.

Every object you bring on stage has to tell you about the circumstances of the character you're playing and the world in which he lives. You have to understand and personalize every object you work with. You have to handle every object imaginatively. You bring a book onto the stage. We have to have some sense of what kind of book it is. Is it a volume of an encyclopedia? Is it the Bible? The way you carry it has to tell us something.

As actors we have to have the ability of children to make believe. A child believes that a stick he has between his legs as he hops up and down is a horse. That indeed is what all acting is made up of — the conviction of the child that the stick is a horse. As an actor you are responsible for this belief. If it's good enough for Dickens, for Balzac, it's good enough for us.

Before using a prop you have to know what the life of the prop is. If you have a gun, you should know how to take it apart, how to clean it, where to put it, how to use it. The gun has its own life, which you have nothing to do with. That life you have to understand as well as a policeman knows the life of his nightstick.

You cannot possibly use a sword unless you study with a specialist for six months. A whole tradition surrounds the wearing of a sword. How do you take it out? How do you put it back in its scabbard? What do you clean steel with? If you don't know how to clean an object and how to put it away, you don't know how to use it.

My brother Luther Adler once played a benefit performance at Madison Square Garden. The action called for him to pick up a gun from a table and shoot a man, but there was no gun on the table. He picked up an imaginary gun and fired it, and the man fell. Because he had this sense of perfection in what he was doing, because he could convince himself, the audience was convinced that a gun had been fired and the shot had killed a man.

In Moscow I watched one of Russia's great actors performing on a stage that was bare except for a stepladder. Seated on the ladder, which was meant to represent the bank of a river, he was supposed to be fishing. There was no pole, no line, no fish hook. But in the way he held his hand and lifted his arm, you could see the pole, the line hanging in the water, the twitch of the line as the fish took hold of the hook. It was genius.

Each prop has its own truth and its own nature. As actors you have to understand every prop. Unfortunately in most young students a sense of giving every prop its dignity does not exist. You cannot use a prop unless you give it dignity and unless you have a liking for it. You must work with it until you know you can use it.

Personalize the props you use by endowing them with some quality that comes from you. Personalize the rose you are about to pin on your dress by shaking drops of water off it or by taking a thorn off its stem. When you put a sweater in a drawer, personalize the sweater by noticing a loose thread and fixing it.

You also have to ask the object what it demands of you. The person who wears a high hat has to know how it lives. The high hat lives in a box, and that box gives you its nature and its value. Do you know how to brush this hat or put it down? Do you know you have to use both hands to put it on? It's made to be worn straight. The person who wears it has a controlled speech, a controlled walk, a controlled mind. You must not bring your own out-of-control culture into the wearing of the hat. In the society of that hat, the human being as well as the clothes were under strict control.

Your job as an actor is to make the world of the play as real as your own, maybe more-so. You're born into your circumstances. If you're ambitious, you can change them, but most of us accept them without thinking.

When you go on stage you can't take anything for granted. You have to examine the circumstances with great care and great understanding. That's the only way you'll feel comfortable there. One of the advantages of concentrating on the circumstances you build on stage is that you won't worry about the audience. When you find yourself worrying about them, it's because you're not absorbed in the world of the play.

▼

The first question an actor has to ask when he steps on the stage is, "Where am I?" When he answers that question carefully. thoughtfully. thoroughly, then he's ready to work. Then there should be no tension about what he's doing. He knows he belongs there, and then he can act. Relaxation comes from the truthfulness of the circumstances the actor creates.

One primary reason many actors feel uncomfortable on stage is that they don't work from the circumstances. They start with the words. The words can tell you about the place, but it's the place that will tell you how to act.

Some of you, I'm sure, are wondering why this is already the sixth class and I haven't given you any scenes to work on. When you begin playing the piano, do you immediately begin studying Beethoven sonatas? Of course not. You begin by working on scales, by making your fingers strong, by understanding harmony. It takes a long time before you're ready to do Beethoven sonatas. The same is true in the theatre.

You're not ready to work with words yet. One of the most important things that you must learn, in fact, is that the play is not in the words. It's behind the words. If you work tirelessly for twenty years without knowing your circumstances, you'll fail. The actor is always in a place. It's his responsibility to understand that place. He doesn't act in mid-air. He has to take the fiction out of the circumstances by letting the place tell him what to do.

You won't behave the same way in the French embassy garden as in the Italian working class garden. You won't dress the same way or even speak or sit the same way.

If you're sipping champagne and nibbling on canapes among people you may not have met but that you know are diplomats and government officials, you're going to be more careful about your posture, about your conversation, about your manners than if you're sitting at a picnic table with a group of people you've known for many years.

I want you to think of something funny that happens in each of these two gardens, something touching, something disturbing, something beautiful.

What's beautiful in the French embassy garden may be the entrance of a diplomat's wife, a very striking woman who's a former movie star and still dresses as if she'll be photographed incessantly. Depending on how you imagine her, that may be more funny than beautiful.

What's beautiful in the Italian garden may be the sound of everyone saying, "Aah," as the hostess comes from the kitchen and places an aromatic plate of pasta on the table. Again, depending on how you imagine her, this too can be funny, though probably in a warmer way than the diplomat's wife.

If the Italian mother is beaming because she's proud of what she's cooked, if she's trying to conceal that pride, we are touched by her modesty. If the French ambassador is making a speech about the heroism of someone he's going to honor and if that person seems uncomfortable about being praised so grandly, we're also touched. In each case what's happening is specific to the circumstances. It doesn't take place in the abstract, but in a specific garden.

One of the most important things to learn is to do as little "acting" as possible. When we let the circumstances dictate what we do, everything will have a reason, will seem perfectly natural, truthful. It's only when we don't understand the circumstances that we have to "act," that we have to fake it. And, believe me, the audience knows that instinctively.

Our job is to make the audience believe the circumstances, but if we're completely absorbed in the world onstage and what we're doing in it, we carry the audience along with us.

The concert pianist doesn't constantly worry about whether the audience will like this or that chord if he plays it a little louder than the scale that led into it. He's not thinking about the audience at all. He's thinking about the music. He understands the logic of the piece he's playing because he's analyzed it and rehearsed it thoroughly. The piece is not just the notes on the printed page but the emotions behind the notes, and the more completely he can express those emotions, the more the audience will share *his* absorption in the piece.

We have to be equally well prepared, as completely absorbed as the pianist. And, just as important, we have to feel the joy is in the doing. If we do it for ourselves and for the play, the audience will be with us completely. The actor has much more fun in acting than the audience does in watching.

Olivier, despite the fact that he was in extremely bad health for many years before he died, never stopped acting. John Gielgud never stops acting. Knowing what it's like on the stage, you would never trade that to be in the audience.

▼

You have to reach the point where acting is pleasurable, not a source of anxiety. A lot of people think of actors as neurotic. That's because the actors they're thinking of are bad actors. There are, after all, actors who love their neuroses. There are,

I'm afraid, teachers who encourage them to dwell on those neuroses. If the students are neurotic, then the teacher looks strong. They become dependent on the teacher, which is something I've never wanted. The teacher becomes a parent, or, even worse, a kind of therapist, always asking, "How do you feel about that?"

It's part of the approach to acting that concentrates on who *you* are, not who the character is. Acting can be the healthiest profession in the world, because it allows you to do things you can't do in real life. It allows you to understand more than just what life provides you. This technique is about doing, not about feeling.

I don't know a great deal about you, but I'm willing to bet none of you is a prince of Denmark. I have the feeling that none of you has become convinced that your father was murdered by your uncle. None of you has a mother that may have been an accomplice to that crime and then married the murderous uncle.

These are very specific circumstances. It is the actor's job to delve into them, to imagine them, not just find circumstances in his own life that correspond to them. There are none. You felt miserable when your beloved grandmother died. You were inconsolable when the dog you had all through your childhood was run over by a car. The memory of these things can give you clues about how Hamlet feels about his father's death, but only clues. Whatever you reconstruct from your emotional memory is no substitute for putting your imagination to work.

When we think about *Hamlet*, the play, we tend to think about the reflective monologues. If we do that, it's easy to imagine it's about what Hamlet's *feeling*. That's only part of it. What makes the part difficult to play is everything that Hamlet *does*. He pretends to be insane. He treats his sweetheart cruelly. Eventually he murders her father and fights a duel with her brother. He arranges for the murder of his schoolchums. He's not just a guy sitting around contemplating suicide. To perform all these actions requires enormous preparation, and it must begin with a sense of the kind of world in which they occur.

▼

Every setting has its own mood. One of the biggest mistakes an actor can make is to "play" mood. If you understand the circumstances, you don't have to "play" the mood. By the way, if you're in a production and you hear the director or the other actors talking about "playing the mood," call your agent immediately. Break your contract. If that's the way they think, it means they have no technique. They're used to faking things, and the play is just not going to work, even if *you* do everything properly. It has to start with the circumstances. There's no other way.

If you've created the interior of a church properly in your imagination, you will have set the mood. A church has its mood. A hospital has its mood. A playground has its mood. A library has its mood. Every bar, whether it's in an expensive hotel or in a seedy neighborhood, has its mood. In creating the physical reality, you will have created the mood.

The more complete the reality you build for yourself, the more thoroughly you understand the *circumstances* of the character and the play, the easier you make it for yourself.

The only time you will be nervous when you go on stage is if you haven't done your preparation — if you pick up a prop and it's just that — a prop, not something with which you have a relationship; or if you look at the set and you haven't created your ideas about it.

If you leave the house without putting your clothes on, you have every reason to be nervous. Going on stage without having built the circumstances is the same thing. You're naked. You have no protection.

The words won't cover you. You may think they're very

THE ART OF ACTING   85

witty or very deep. It doesn't matter. They will seem transparent. They will seem hollow if they do not come out of the circumstances. If the play is just about the words, the audience can stay home and read the text. The reason they come to the theatre is to experience the life the actor brings to the words.

We should be grateful we live in a time when the general imagination has been impoverished, a time when people read novels that are neither very rich nor very deep, when they go to movies aimed at the mentality of teenage boys, when they watch endless television banalities, all of which accustoms them to a very trivial kind of entertainment. They're used to very routine cooking — macaroni and cheese. They're happy with "fast food." You're in a position to give them banquets. That's your great opportunity.

Your curse is that you have chosen a form that requires endless study. Your job is to know what political time a play is set in, what class the characters are in, what style the play is written in. This doesn't mean you have to go to Harvard. It doesn't mean you have to spend the rest of your life taking classes at the Stella Adler Conservatory.

It means you have to read, you have to observe, you have to think, so that when you turn your imagination on, it has the fuel to do its job. When you handle a prop, you're not just "Handling a prop" — the object speaks to you, and you can make the object something that helps the audience understand the play. That's what your job is. If you can't convey a deep understanding of the play to the audience, then acting is just a joke, a form of self-indulgence.

The few hours you spend here every week should be just the tip of the iceberg. If you've learned anything so far, it should be how important it is to observe and to observe in detail. What you observe and what you imagine constitute your armor as actors. They're what keep you from ever being on stage naked. How strong and protective that armor becomes is up to you.

GETTING HOLD OF ACTING'S CONTROLS

You've come here to learn to act, but I want to teach you *not* to act. If somebody tells you they loved the way you acted, I hope you know that means you've failed.

If a fellow actor tells you what you're doing is *indicating*, it's his way of saying you're faking, and that's the worst thing anybody can say.

A hundred years ago audiences were much more willing to accept artifice than they are today. The verb people used then to describe what actors did was "play." People used to say they were going to see Sir Henry Irving *play*. Nowadays you hear actors say they're going to watch Al Pacino *work*.

Nowadays we don't want artificiality. We want realism, and that's why if the audience thinks you're *acting*, you've failed them. What you have to learn is to perform actions, because if you're performing an action, you're doing something. You're not *indicating*, you're doing.

Our job is to study actions, to analyze them, to find their anatomy, their spine. When we study a script, we're trying to find what *actions* it requires of us. When we're performing these actions — whether it be "to teach" or "to learn" or "to escape" or "to pray" or "to beg" — we communicate the nature of the action to the audience.

If we truly do these actions, we don't have to worry about "acting." If we're actually doing something, we don't have to worry about faking.

Let's not even use the word acting. Let's start by talking about "controls." When you use a control, it changes the nature of everything you do. It forces you to act in a certain way. They simplify your task. You can't play "old." You can't play "young." But you can find physical controls that will make you seem old or young.

One simple exercise is to lean on your heels, then put on a pair of glasses and peer over them. That will immediately give you the appearance of being old. Before you can bring that on the stage, however, you have to understand how leaning on your heels affects the rest of your body, how it controls your posture, how it affects the way you move.

As an actor you have to be acutely aware of everything about your body. You need to become muscularly facile in your work. You need to memorize what muscles control the actions you perform. Equally important, you need to learn how much muscular exertion each action requires.

If, for example, I pick up a metal folding chair and hold it away from my body, what muscles do I use? They are not the muscles in my legs or in my neck. They are mostly the muscles in my fingertips. How much effort does it require? Not a great deal.

If you pick up a log and hold it in your arms you use a different set of muscles. It requires certain muscles in your hands, your wrists, your arms, your shoulders. You must memorize what muscles you use and what effort the action takes, obviously much more than the metal chair.

You must repeat it often enough with a real log that you can then pick up an imaginary one. The memory of how to do it and how much effort it takes should be in your body. If you prepare properly, that memory stays there and is ready for action whenever you need it.

Let's return to that jar whose lid has been fastened too tightly. Which muscles does it require? How much effort does it take? Do it again and again. Now do it with an imaginary jar. If you've done it carefully with the real jar, your muscles will remember how to do it with an imaginary one. Do the same thing with a stuck door.

In rehearsal, and often even in performance, actors will find themselves in circumstances that are half real and half imaginary. This is where muscular memory will prove extremely useful.

By taking a physical control you're letting your body dictate ways to move. If you're concentrating on what your body is telling you, you're doing something that is truthful. You're not "acting." You're not "indicating." You're not "faking" anything.

▼

Let's start with a vocal control. To affect a lisp, put your tongue at the back of your teeth and say the following sentence: "She was a very stunning girl, and she was walking up the street, and she stopped to look at the shop window." You must be able to locate where the lisp comes from.

Learning the lisp is the beginning of learning how to manage accents. Every accent requires an adjustment of the way your tongue forms words. Once you find these adjustments you have a way to control the accent. You're not just doing an imitation.

Go to a neighborhood where people speak with an accent. Identify two vowels and one consonant that determine the accent. Write a little speech for a character in that neighborhood. Now write it a second time altering the two vowels and the consonant every time they appear. Read the second version aloud until you feel absolutely comfortable and natural with the accent.

Another good exercise is to take a physical control like a lisp or an accent and recite a poem using it. To do this properly the control must be so "second nature" to you that you can concentrate on the text.

An actor must be in control of every part of his body.

When I work on my voice I allow nothing to interrupt me — no telephone calls, no messages, no appointments. An actor has to work all the time so he is prepared to accept any challenge the theatre offers him, so that he can perform in all the styles of the theatre, from the Greeks to Shakespeare to the moderns.

An actor has to be sufficiently in control of his body that he can play many different kinds of people. You must learn to control your body so you can perform movements you are not used to and develop ways of walking that are right for the characters you're playing.

Take a particular physical control of the body, a stiff knee, for example, or a bent back, and locate it and the muscles that support and control it. You have to understand the control so completely, you have to have worked with it so thoroughly that it becomes second nature to you, to the point that you do it totally unconsciously.

Firs, the old family servant in Chekhov's *The Cherry Orchard*, walks with a bent back. The actor who plays him has to know the history of the back — how and under what circumstances it happened. Steps were taken to correct the injury, and he must know them. The actor must exercise constant care in the way he moves about. In time he learns to work with his infirmity and live with it. When he puts his coat on he must be careful. He has been conditioned to be careful.

▼

Let's work on physical controls by taking something very simple, a stiff knee. We see how a stiff knee affects the way we walk, the way we sit. Take this simple control and see if you can make it an inseparable part of your routine — for an hour, for an afternoon, for a day. See if you can live with it. That means taking a bath with it, going up steps with it, lying down with it. If you can't live with the control for at least a few hours a day — or if it tires you out — you're not ready to take it on stage.

The important thing to remember is that you must make the control seem normal. Let's go back to our vocal control, the lisp — a person with a lisp doesn't want you to be conscious of it. He tries to communicate as clearly as possible, to overcome his lisp, not to emphasize it.

The same is true of the physical control, the stiff knee. The person for whom the stiff knee is an integral part of his life tries to move as normally as he can. He doesn't want you to be constantly aware of it. Nevertheless it affects his every movement. You have to be aware of how it affects the whole body, but you must be able to register those effects un-selfconsciously.

In Clifford Odets' play *Awake and Sing* my brother Luther Adler played a character with a wooden leg. The entire world believed that Luther had only one leg. That's because he completely mastered how a one-legged man moves.

You can build up this ability by starting with simple exercises. Perform three everyday actions having to do with food preparation or eating with two fingers stiff. Memorize the muscles needed to perform an everyday task in the kitchen. After performing the task enough times to develop a "muscular memory," do the task without the object.

Exercises like this will sensitize your awareness of how your body performs. The body is never in a straight line. You must be able to stand on one foot and keep the other foot light. In this position one shoulder is down, the other up. The curve of the body is very subtle. When the body bends, see where the knee bends, and see how that affects the other foot. Notice how the strength is always in one place, and the other is relaxed.

The more you're aware of how your body behaves under normal circumstances the better you'll make adjustments to the specific circumstances of a play.

The position of your body also has a great influence on your voice. Certain positions have great strength in them, and they allow the voice to project. If you think of yourself as being a piece of marble statuary and say the line, "I will kill you," how much more voice do you have? Say the line, "I'll throw a stone" in your normal voice. Now become a marble statue and say it again. How much more powerful your voice becomes when you turn into a statue!

When you become *somebody* and say, "I'll throw a stone," it could be Moses speaking, because you have theatricalized yourself and turned into marble. Marble has the property of eternity. That's where you get the power to say, "Friends, Romans, countrymen, lend me your ears!"

An intense speech like Marc Antony's in *Julius Caesar* must be performed with all the emotion and tension in the words, but, since acting is based on a lack of tension, you must do it in a state of relaxation. That comes when you're entirely comfortable with your body and what your body can do.

▼

Everything I've been saying to you today has had a certain logic to it, an orderliness, yes, a sense of method. But I never want you to have the feeling that acting is a profession for book-keepers. That's why the term The Method has become so odious. It implies that acting is an utterly sensible, organized activity. You do step one, step two, step three and, *voila*! You're not an accountant any more, you're an actor. If it were that reasonable we would have even more actors than we already do.

That's why at this point I want to introduce animal exercises. Go to the zoo and study an animal. Study the way it moves and the noises it makes. Observe the life of the monkey so that you can duplicate some of its moves.

We're all bound by social conventions. They give us a shield to hide behind. The purpose of the animal exercises is to rid the actor of his social mask and to free him from his inhibitions. To become an animal, to make non-human movements and noises reduces the actor's fear of making a fool of himself. I want you to experience the freedom of the stage, to dare to do anything.

Learn to screech like a monkey. Make bird calls. Roar like a lion. Lose your inhibitions, free your talent. Use yourself to the maximum.

As an animal, you must know who you are but not how you'll react. Being an animal teaches you about spontaneity. If you're scared, do something. If you're hungry, do something. Always be specific, never general, and do everything to the maximum. That's why it's dangerous to be on a stage with an animal — they always do things to the maximum.

The same was true of Zero Mostel. That's why I used to warn my students never to get on a stage with an animal, a child or Zero Mostel.

As an animal, you have a firm sense of your identity, which gives you the grounding from which you can behave spontaneously. If you're a kitten, you are curious, but also timid, afraid of larger animals. If you're a pigeon, you mind your own business, observe and escape from danger.

Becoming an animal is an extremely useful exercise. Build a program for yourself whereby every day you do fifteen minutes of animal sounds and bird calls. This will teach you to use your voice differently. It will also make you aware of sounds you didn't know you could make.

One of Laurence Olivier's most memorable roles was the title character in *Titus Andronicus*, one of the few plays people would prefer to think Shakespeare did *not* write. It is a play full of gruesome events and overheated poetry.

Nevertheless a great actor can turn even a bad play into something unforgettable. No one who saw Olivier's performance as Titus ever forgot the bloodcurdling scream he uttered. He once explained that this scream came from imagining he was an ermine. These are little animals prized for their fur. You have to catch them in a way that doesn't harm their fur.

The way ermine are caught is by pouring salt on ice. When the ermine licks the salt his tongue sticks to the ice and he's trapped. Olivier's scream came from the realization he'd been trapped.

Imitating an animal will teach you an enormous amount about your body. To lope like a monkey requires great freedom. It also requires great agility. Every animal has its own way of moving, and the more you can recreate these movements, the greater will be the range of your movements overall.

When you feel you have control of your body, move your hips a little, being careful not to move your knees or your shoulders. Just your hips. Your ability to control this shift is a good test of your professionalism.

All of these exercises have a point beyond themselves. When you use a vocal control, when you use a physical control, when you imitate an animal, it forces you to look at the world from a different perspective. It also forces you to move and speak differently. In every case you are responding to very specific circumstances. If you respond truthfully, there will be nothing fake about your acting.

A character doesn't consist of how he feels but in what he does. Feeling comes from doing.

LEARNING ACTIONS

In the modern theatre, which began in the late 19th century, there's no more important action than "to discuss."

In the theatre that begins with Ibsen a play must have at least two ideas of equal importance — two points of view. More important than that, two truths. The play sets these truths before the audience with equal weight, and the audience must decide for itself which to accept. At the end of *A Doll's House*, when Nora has announced her intention of leaving Torvald, he tells her, "Your first duty is to your husband and your children." She tells him, "No, my first duty is to myself."

For the audience that first saw the play Nora's declaration was shocking. We take it in stride, but the play only works if we feel that Torvald's idea of duty and Nora's idea of duty both have value. We tend to side with Nora. If that is the case, there's no play because there's no struggle.

The audience must be urged first toward one idea, then toward the other, so that when they leave the theatre they're still wrestling with the ideas.

In many modern playwrights it is extremely important that the actors be able to discuss ideas. To understand the action "to discuss," however, it's helpful to start with other actions, "to talk," "to chat," and "to converse."

▼

"To talk" is the most basic form of communication. We talk all the time without taking it seriously. In daily life we talk about serious things that mean nothing to us — the national economy or international politics.

We spend our whole lives talking about these things without really experiencing them. Also, when we talk we don't listen carefully. Another characteristic of talk is that we constantly interrupt each other.

Choose a partner and talk about painting the dirty walls or repairing the broken light fixtures or fixing the sofa. The tone should be matter-of-fact, straightforward, but without emotion.

"To chat" is close to our everyday conversation, but it's not matter of fact. It has a deliberate lightness, as you can see in the noun from which the verb *chat* is drawn, *chitchat*. Most of the time we're not discussing ideas, we're not even talking about practical matters. We're chatting. "Oh, what a lovely hat. That shade of blue is perfect with your dress."

Even when we ask each other, "How are you?" we really don't care. It's a conversation starter. That's why we never answer, "It's interesting you should ask, I have the oddest pain in my left ankle." Most of the time we just say, "I'm fine. How are you?"

Another way of describing "to chat" is to say you're "shooting the breeze." That's a way of saying that chatting is pleasant, it's polite, it's airy, it's light, but it's empty. It doesn't matter. Nothing depends on it. It's a way to pass the time.

In fact "to chat" is a fake action. As I leave my apartment to get into the car, the driver already knows I'm not in a mood for contact. I say, "Nice to see you." And he's already driving off. He knows it doesn't matter. It's normal. It's fake.

That's why it bothers me to chat. I do it, but it's an action you can't control, so I try to avoid it in life, just as I avoid gossip. The point of gossip is to escalate what I want to say, make what I say seem more important than it is by giving it a secretive quality, as if what I'm telling you no one else must know.

It's a good exercise consciously "to chat." It's like the exercises we did to develop muscular memory. What we were doing then was getting our physical muscles accustomed to the different weights of things. Here we're getting our mental muscles accustomed to the different weights of kinds of conversation. There's no heavy lifting in chatting. It's as light as can be.

Of course for some of you, who are unacquainted with any kind of conversation, even chatting may not be so easy. Take a partner and "chat." Remember, it's a form of verbal badminton. It doesn't require as much energy or skill or effort as tennis. It's just bouncing the shuttlecock back and forth.

▼

The next step in our progression toward "to discuss" is "to converse." Like "to chat," "to converse" is on the light level. It's airy, it's polite. It doesn't have much more gravity than "to chat," but it has particular social circumstances. It implies the middle or the upper class.

When you're seated at a formal dinner party with people you may or may not know it's possible that you'll develop enough rapport that your conversation will be on the level of "to discuss," but more than likely you have no particular desire to reach the other person. You're not trying to persuade this stranger. There's no reason to be intimate. You listen, you answer. You don't interrupt.

It's not as impersonal as "to chat," nor does it have any great depth. The ability to converse is a social skill, a way of behaving in a friendly manner with someone you don't really know, but also deliberately keeping your distance.

It used to be that when you were on an airplane next to a stranger you would "chat" or "converse" as a way of passing the time. It was a way of being friendly, of being civil, but it didn't lead to any great intimacy or intellectual depth. It was a way of not going deep.

Nowadays people on airplanes are barely civil. They have their books or their magazines and behave as if they were alone.

▼

Once we can distinguish the gradations between "to talk," "to chat" and "to converse," we're ready to tackle "to discuss." Discussion of ideas is at the center of the modern theatre. In every great play from Ibsen on, one finds what we call the discussive element.

From Shaw and O'Casey to Beckett and Pinter, from O'Neill and Odets to Arthur Miller, Tennessee Williams and Edward Albee, the modern, naturalistic theatre is a theatre of ideas, a theatre whose purpose is to make an audience think and learn about the larger questions of life.

If two people simply agree on the stage, then we're finished. There's no play and nothing more to say. The modern theatre is based on our ability to consider two points of view. In a play, in any dramatic situation, I may be a proponent of the idea under discussion and my partner may be against it. Torvald is for Nora's duty to him and her family. Nora is for her duty to herself. Two contradictory ideas are expressed, and it's up to the audience either to choose between them or to decide on some other course of action. When the discussion is over, nobody wins.

The discussive element entered the theatre when the rise of the middle class brought an end to the easily identified and widely accepted values of morality — manners and ethics that were a part of a more sharply defined class structure. The middle class has only pick-up values. Their lack of certitude means that for every question there are two sides. Consequently, in the modern theatre there is no one truth.

In discussion one must recognize the difference between issues of varying weight and importance, between an issue such as the inevitability of death and the question of which presidential candidate to vote for, and judge as between the larger and the smaller issue.

I can take the opinion that New York is overcrowded, and that issue can be raised to a higher level, bringing in another point of view: overcrowding is in the nature of city life. Every city in the world is going to have an escalation of population. One can accept this as a positive or hope for overpopulation's brutal correctives — disease, attrition and death. In theatre the interest comes from having an opinion. You may have one opinion as a person, another in the theatre.

When you start a discussion such as urban overpopulation, you must stick to the topic and not wander into other epic ideas. You have no right to go far afield or to be general.

The first thing that distinguishes the action "to discuss" from all the other forms of conversation ("to talk," "to chat" or "to converse") is the relationship to the partner. In these other styles you may or may not know your partner. It doesn't matter because the bond between you never solidifies.

To have a true discussion both partners must be serious about the issues. This is the first action in which content really matters. It's not just a way of passing the time or being polite or sharing impersonal information.

Each partner has a very definite point of view, but he listens to the other person carefully. He may not change his opinion, but he listens. This is not chatting, not conversing, not talking. This is discussion.

In a discussion both partners must take a genuine interest in the ideas. Discussion should take place on a mutually interesting subject. As an actor you have to be able to take either side.

If you can't take both sides, it means you can only play yourself.

There's no more important exercise than taking a side on some big issue, like the necessity of legalizing abortion, and then taking the other side and arguing it so effectively that a listener can't tell which side you really favor.

In a genuine discussion there's no need to win. In a discussion you don't need to cut off your partner. The ideas expressed by your partner should excite you. The exchange should stimulate you.

In this action, as in almost no other in the field of communication, there's genuine understanding. The give-and-take is real and unforced. It's perhaps the most important action in modern playwriting because the audience understands both sides of the discussion and becomes the third partner in the play. The members of the audience can leave the theatre and make up their own minds.

All right, let's choose partners and discuss the question: Should a man be a family man or an artist? Should a woman be an actress or a wife and mother? Let's take a few minutes and organize our thoughts and then we'll begin. Who'd like to go first? All right, Hillary and Bob.

BOB: Being an actor is a full-time job. So is being a father. A man has to choose. With women it's different. Only women can have children.

HILLARY: No, Bob. That's wrongheaded and sexist. I feel . . .

STELLA: Sweetheart, I have to interrupt you. You are not interested in what he's saying. You're anxious to talk. That's not discussion. Discussion comes out of what your partner says, not what you feel.

I don't want to know how you *feel*. I want to know that you can justify saying that Art is more important to you than anything. I want you to be able to say, "I have something in me that will not permit me to be tied down."

The artists who succeed are the ones who understand that these themes are universal, not personal. It has nothing to do with whether *you* like it or you don't if a woman is better off bringing up a family. That idea is thousands of years old. It starts with God.

The level of discussion has got to be on a higher level. It has to be on the level of what these two things bring to the world. It's too informative. You give a lot of information but it's without heart.

What I call the agitation isn't there. Don't open your mouth unless you *have* to . . . from inside.

You think your beauty will help you. It won't help your art. It'll help you get ahead, but your art comes from somewhere else. Either what we do matters or it doesn't. If it matters we can't let our personal pride get in the way.

Now you didn't give your partner much chance to speak. He was just beginning to present his ideas. If only one side of the discussion is presented the audience is going to know what they're expected to think. They must understand two sides of an idea. Discussion should change the audience's point of view or at least make them think twice about what they felt beforehand. They go home and come to a new understanding.

Discussion is not just about the ideas. If that were all that mattered we could just read two essays or have two essays read to us. We have to experience the give and take of the two participants.

Neither of you should start talking by announcing the topic. That's what happens in a formal debate. Everything you say has to have some emotional content. Before you speak, imagine that you've been provoked by a specific statement. Hear it and then react. Even when you begin, you must react.

Whoever speaks second has to make clear what made him

start to talk. He's not there just to present the arguments he rehearsed beforehand. We have to feel everything you say is prompted by something you've heard. Don't start from yourself. Start with, What did your partner say that made *you* say I don't agree with that?

Otherwise we have a false situation — a situation where the action starts with your talking. It has to start before you talk.

All right, let's try it again.

JOHN: Artists must be aloof from society, aloof from a family . . .

STELLA: I'm afraid I have to stop you. That's an intellectual idea you're presenting, and you're not an intellectual, God knows. You have to find a way of presenting ideas, justifying them so that we can believe they come from you, not from something you read.

The question of whether an actor or an actress should marry is not an intellectual one. On each side you can make several points. You can say acting is an insecure profession whereas marriage is stable and enduring. You can say the actor especially needs the support of another human being, and that actors have a great capacity for love.

Don't raise any of these points unless you understand them and they awaken you. Take ideas that will provoke the other person to a response. On the other side, you can say that since actors are never secure, they make poor partners in a marriage, and no woman would want to marry an actor.

An actor, furthermore, must devote all his time to his profession. The career of an actor doesn't permit a family or the responsibilities that marriage and children entail.

This argument goes to the very heart of why acting is an important profession, one that commands the whole of the actor's being.

▼

Every actor I know walks out on a set and wants to kill himself because he doesn't know how to make the play live. They never lose that anxiety. But you want to make things yours right away. You can't. The only thing you can produce immediately is fake acting. You've got to get used to it slowly. And you've got to make yourself bigger.

I was married to Harold Clurman, who was the greatest man in the American theatre, who practically founded the American theatre. I was married to Mitchell Wilson, who was the assistant to Enrico Fermi in the development of the atom bomb.

I didn't go for the small fry. I didn't because I didn't want to live that way. I was brought up by my father, and in our home there was no small talk at all.

You can't go on the stage unless you're filled with things that give you life all day long . . . and *problems* all day long, ones that develop you.

Discussion is a hard action for you to grasp because it's a very civilized action. In this country we don't discuss. We argue. We're like taxi drivers. Our national temperament is intolerant of listening.

The action "to argue" grows out of the action "to discuss." It's when you hear your partner but you don't hear. You understand? You continue with what you think. Argument has passion. It's not about logic and mind.

The next stage after "to argue" is "to fight." "To fight" means there is no control, and very little listening. You attack in all directions. "To fight" is to go after something with no waiting.

From arguing to fighting is a natural progression, and with fighting we've reached the end of the chain of communicating.

MAKING ACTIONS DOABLE

A t this stage in the technique you're developing a vocabulary of actions. Everything is based on actions. An actor develops a character from the things he does. That's why the actor must understand actions.

Every action you do has its *nature*, its truth. In order to be truthful onstage you must know the nature of what you're doing, and it must be truthfully done. Everything has to have its logic. It must have truth, growth (progression) and a beginning, middle and end (sequence). A play is made intelligible to an audience through the actor's actions, a series of separate but logically connected physical or psychological activities that breathe life into the play and create the moment-by-moment truth.

In modern plays, the playwright provides only an outline or skeleton. It's up to you to add flesh and blood, to make the playwright's ideas lucid. The content of the play can only be brought to life through your actions.

It's not words that make a performance. Even the best actor cannot put into words everything he knows, for what the well-prepared and thoughtful actor knows about his character is a hundred times more complicated than the words in the playscript. It can only be seen as action.

When we study actions there are three ways to go about it. The first is to ask, Have I done this action? The second is to ask,

Have I seen this action done? If the answer to both those questions is no, the third approach, and in some ways the most important, is to go to the imagination.

We've already worked on reproducing certain movements, like opening the tight lid of a bottle. We trained our muscles to see just how much effort was required, so that we didn't exaggerate it when we reproduced it without the object.

These seem like little things, but they're important. In acting these tiny physical things have to be comfortable for the body. One thing that makes a young actor very uncomfortable is he skims over something, or he indicates it. It's a part of your technique that you must not skim over, not *indicate* physical truths that the activity needs. Do you agree to that?

Opening a bottle is a very simple task, but it's a very educational one. You have to open a . . . you have a bottle . . . ooh, God, that's strong. But then it comes open. If you open the bottle, strangely enough, if you really open the bottle, that which is difficult is easier, because you've really opened the bottle. Do you understand?

If you haven't really opened the bottle, then that next tiny moment of — *phuh!* — won't come. Is that clear to you? It's a trick, that when the body is true, the soul reacts. When the body lies, the soul gets frightened. The way to be sure you're being truthful is to focus on these tiny truths.

All activity is complicated. If I say to you, "Write something down in your book," you have to reach for the book and find the page. That's the nature of life. Now all these complications have to be true on the stage. These physical, small things have to be true. Now write this in your head: no physical activity with all its little truths can be done without rehearsal. They cannot be done. When you get very expert, maybe you can do them. But at this moment you *cannot* do them.

Whether you're building a fire or making coffee or ironing a shirt or packing a bag, all require that every little part of the action be true. The inside of every action has to be done truthfully. You cannot indicate it. You cannot indicate those little truths, just as you cannot indicate looking at the audience or talking to people. You can't indicate it. It must happen.

As long as your objectives are small and manageable, they're in your control. When you're in control you can bring life to what you're doing.

I went to Wilmington over the weekend, and there was a little girl with me. She had the instinct to fight boredom, and in that respect children are great actors. She would say, "Oooh, we're in the dark now." Then she'd say, "Now we're coming into the light." She didn't say, in a monotone, "We're in the dark now and we're coming into the light," because she didn't want to take the life out of it.

Grownups take the life out of things. It's better to make things up, to use the imagination, than to kill them.

When you start work on a physical action, don't start with the performance. Say to yourself, I'm the director. Let me fool around with this and see if I have it, because I don't want to do it for an audience unless it's easy.

▼

Let's take the physical activity washing clothes in a stream. The first thing is to build the circumstances of the stream itself. Is it on the edge of a deserted lot? Is it in the middle of a forest? That's just the beginning.

It might be useful to practice the action of washing clothes in the bathtub. That will give you the experience, but it's not enough. Think about the soap. It gets onto the thing you're washing, and then it gets dipped in the water. That's the kind of tiny task that can grow every time you do it. You have to make everything your own, come alive. That's the difference between what you did in the bathtub and what you do on stage.

I'm washing a slip in the stream, and I see that the water is muddy. I take the slip out to wait for the water to become clear. The stream is alive, terribly alive to me. It's sparkling and it's clear, and it's wonderful. Oh, but this part is all milky. I'm not going to wash my slip until the water becomes clear again.

I love my stream because the stream is alive. Everything happens out of the stream. You mustn't let the stream stay pedestrian. You mustn't let the stream *not* partake of the life of what you're doing.

Study building a fire. It's not something you can do randomly. You can't just take a match to a log and expect the fire to catch or last. You have to start with something small, strips of paper. On top of the paper you can put twigs or kindling wood, small branches. The fire has to build. You have to have the smaller things catch, and they'll light the larger ones. The log is on top, and it won't begin to burn until everything underneath is crackling.

Every physical activity is like this. You have to understand its logic. You have to make it doable. People don't act in real life. They experience one moment, then the next. They react to circumstances. The actor's job is to make the circumstances in which he moves on stage so lively, so immediate that they enliven his actions.

There are strong and weak actions. To be strong, an action needs an end, an objective. If I say, "I'd like to drink something," that's a weak action. If I say, "I'd like to drink coffee," that's a strong one. There must be an end, an objective, or else the action is weak. "I'm leaving" is weak. "I'm leaving this room" is strong. "I'd like to go somewhere" is weak. "I'd like to take a walk in the park" is strong.

Building an imaginary fire teaches us that every action has its own logic. Practice activities such as setting the table or sorting the mail. The basics of setting the table are easy enough. You put down the glasses. You put down the plates. You put down the forks and spoons. You fold the napkins. But when we do these things on stage the action cannot be as mundane as in real life, where no one cares if you're boring. On stage you cannot afford to be boring even for one instant, and therein lies the difference between real time and stage time — between how long it takes to do what you actually do in life and how long it should take to represent what you do in life on the stage.

In life an action is worth exactly the amount of time it takes to do it. On stage, where thirty years of a person's life are compressed into two and a half hours, it is never worth that much time. So the actor, in performing simple activities such as writing a letter or reading a book or sewing on a button, constantly needs to ask, how much is it worth?

The technique for making real time fit into stage time we call smartening up the action, which means shortening what you do, trimming it, editing it, so that the audience, while understanding fully what you're doing, won't feel you've gone on for too long. The audience will always be the best judge, but an actor has to anticipate their reactions.

Smartening up an action requires pre-planning. If I need to smoke a cigarette, the pack is already open and one or two cigarettes are sticking out. I cannot be caught on stage fumbling for a cigarette, unless it's a choice.

If I have to look up a telephone number in the H's, I start thumbing through the book hunting for the H's, and it takes too long. I need to arrange myself so that I know exactly what page I'm going to. Then I read a few names, and when I come to the one I want I put a pencil mark next to it. I have conveyed the truth of the action quickly and truthfully. In a book, if I have to get to page 460, I place a match between the pages to get there quickly.

If I'm sitting at a makeup table, I can put on mascara, lipstick, eye shadow, powder, and, while this is completely realistic, it takes much too long for the stage. You simply fix on your lipstick, wipe one eyebrow, and you're done. Unlike life, you don't have a lifetime on stage. You must smarten actions up by selecting one or two telling parts.

▼

Last time we went through a series of actions that involve talking, to chat, to discuss, to argue, to fight. An action one encounters repeatedly in modern theatre is "to reminisce," a device playwrights commonly use to introduce poetry or poetic prose. A retreat into a more favorably remembered past, reminiscing is itself a means of escape from the sometimes unbearable realities of the present.

To reminisce is to soliloquize, to recall the past and bring it back to life. It's different from remembering, which is automatic and associated with daily life. You remember your telephone number and your grocery store list. You remember to answer a letter.

In reminiscence, a man brings back what he loves. You can say, "One day I was walking along a river. It was flowing quietly. It was a lovely day. I sat in the shade. It was very quiet. I could see the mountains. I looked up at the sky." When you reminisce, you can sense how little physical movement is required. When you use a lot of words, you don't need a lot of gestures.

The anatomy of the action "to reminisce" is to relive the experience, to see again what you once saw and to remember it fondly. When you start to reminisce, you lose the world. This table I'm sitting at no longer exists for me, only the river I walked along that spring day under a cloudless sky through a mountainous valley.

When I reminisce, I become detached and my words take on a poetic quality. To reminisce is to reinvent the world. Remembering is simply experiencing it all over again, which is closer to description.

Description can be expressed in gesture by a chopping motion of the hand. The gesture of reminiscence is a gentler, freer flowing, wave-like motion of the hand. When you reminisce everything becomes significant because it's gone.

Reminiscence loses the present world and recreates a time in the past. It is a giving over to a life that has disappeared but still lives in you. Time makes it more significant. Life becomes more terrible or more beautiful. When you have that life, in your reminiscence, you don't need this present one. Reminiscence deals with something long ago that meant a change in your life. This action cannot be in any sense casual. It must be on a high level.

To reminisce is different from telling a story. "When I was little, I had the opportunity to go to England . . ." That's telling, not creating. This is one of the few actions in which the partner doesn't matter. Not caring whether the partner hears him or not, the actor tries to bring back something lost, which only he can make live again.

Reminiscing has in it longing, pain and loss. Set on a dark level, it is neither light nor cheerful. Among the lost moments in Blanche DuBois' life in *A Streetcar Named Desire* is this:

"He was a boy, just a boy, when I was a very young girl. When I was sixteen, I made the discovery — love. All at once and much, much too completely. It was like you suddenly turned a blinding light on something that had always been half in shadow, that's how it struck the world for me. But I was unlucky. Deluded. There was something different about the boy, a nervousness, a softness and tenderness which wasn't like a man's, although he wasn't the least bit effeminate looking — still — that thing was there . . . "

The principle of reminiscing is not to memorize the text, but to mark the sequences of the thought. Don't act and don't make believe. Take time to go into the reminiscence and re-experience it. As an inner monologue, it doesn't need a partner. In Robert's monologue in the first act of Eugene O'Neill's *Beyond the Horizon*, the theme is the big dream of life, of reaching the sea and experiencing its mysterious force.

In rehearsing the action of reminiscing, the necessary steps are first to create the background for the reminiscence and make it your own. The reminiscence has a sequence of ideas. Paraphrase the sequence so that the ideas are in you, not in the words. Fill in the sequence with your own words without the text in order to make the words of the author belong to you.

Before starting the reminiscence, walk around the stage. But don't walk anywhere without going somewhere. Don't begin without a starting image, say of an object on the stage, from the couch or the table. You start from a place, then you move beyond it. You get the starting impulse from the object, then you dismiss the couch or the table so we can feel the isolation of your mind, your removal to another time and place. To interrupt the monotony of the reminiscence, you break from it, returning to the room and to the present, before going back again to the reminiscence.

In Robert's reminiscence in *Beyond the Horizon*, he acknowledges the presence of the adoring Ruth and addresses her directly:

"So I used to stare out over the fields to the hills, out there — and somehow after a time I'd forget any pain I was in, and start dreaming. I knew the sea was over beyond those hills — the folks had told me — and I used to wonder what the sea was like, and try to form a picture of it in my mind. There was all the mystery in the world to me then about that — far-off sea — and there still is! It called to me then just as it does now. And other times my eyes would follow this road, winding off into the distance, toward the hills, as if it, too, was searching for the sea. And I'd promise myself that when I grew up and was strong, I'd follow that road, and it and I would find the sea together. You see, my making this trip is only keeping that promise of long ago."

In the stage direction O'Neill says Ruth (who says, "Yes, I see,") is "charmed by his low musical voice telling the dreams of his childhood."

Robert continues:

"Those were the only happy moments of my life then, dreaming there at the window. I like to be all alone — those times. I got to know all the different kinds of sunsets by heart. And all those sunsets took place over there — beyond the horizon. So gradually I came to believe that all the wonders of the world happened on the other side of those hills."

In this soliloquy, Robert is struggling to make himself clear and groping to find the sources of his life. Like all human beings at one time or another, he resists the attachment to reality and longs to return to the primal source of life, which is the sea — to live life more instinctually.

To reminisce is not by itself an action. An action, to be an action, has to contain some of the content. You don't simply reminisce. You reminisce about something, something you care about. You can reminisce about your lost home. You can reminisce about the family that has scattered.

A lost family prompts the most affecting of reminiscences even today when family life, for all practical purposes, hardly exists. Today, at eighteen, children leave home to return only for an occasional visit. Most of the students I teach have drifted away. But family life can be imagined through texts such as John Van Druten's *I Remember Mama*.

Here is Katrin recalling her family:

"It's funny, but when I look back, I always see Nels and Christine and myself looking almost as we do today. I guess that's because the people you see all the time stay the same age in your head. Dagmar's different. She was always the baby — so I see her as a baby. Even Mama — it's funny, but I always see Mama as around forty. She couldn't always have been forty."

When they study this text, students try to create the period out of their imagination by describing the kind of clothes Mama would have worn — the skirt, the blouse, the decorations, the jewelry, the shoes, when "every Saturday night Mama would sit down by the kitchen table and count out the money Papa had brought home in the little envelope."

In paraphrasing a monologue, you must have specific pictures in mind. Rather than words, always in preference to words, start with a place. If you're at a beach, what at the beach will help you remember Mama? Start with seashells. Do something that will get you in the mood. The family's all gone now. In your reminiscence you must bring them back together.

The objects you choose can help or hinder you. A radio, for example, something mechanical, is a mistake. Instead, turn to nature. A radio leaves you stone cold inside.

For example, I remember one student finding a simple bottle of beer unhelpful. Paraphrasing from William Saroyan's *The Time of Your Life*, about childhood on an Ohio farm, he seated himself at a table on the stage. Placing a bottle of beer and a stein in front of him, he poured half of the bottle into the stein, took a sip and began his monologue about the family losing the farm in the Depression and being forced to move to the city.

At the appropriate time he broke from the monologue and addressed his partner in an everyday tone of voice, "That's when we moved to Chicago." Then he returned to the detached state of reminiscence again. But the beer and the stein, for the delicate personal nature of his reminiscence, were too ordinary. The beer fed his stomach but not his reminiscence.

Students seem reluctant to take on material that has size. They seem unwilling to go to a tragic level, to recognize in the ordinary facts of a story, as in the passage above, the larger truths, such as a man's need for a home, the sad destruction of a family, the transience of life.

Wordsworth said, "Poetry is emotion recollected in tranquility." Bringing that poetic quality into it, you reminisce about your high school graduation. "There it was that day! There was — an auditorium!" You don't try to make it natural. So you don't try to bring it back to a natural tone of voice. "Was there a graduation? Was there? There's the apple tree. There's the haywagon."

You must not bring it into your reality. It must exist in tranquility. You must see if you can recreate this lost world. As a large poetic action, reminiscing is done only by people who cannot bear this world.

Reminiscence is related to dreaming. In both actions you lose the sense of your body, but you can't try too hard to achieve the effect or go too fast. You must make it come alive for the first time. It's the miracle of *Our Town*. A running child, an apple tree — they have died and you're bringing them back. The human being is given this one extra dimension, his memory of the past, and this one extra dimension is peculiarly available to the stage.

Reminiscence has in it a miracle. "And they were alive . . ." The miracle of life — it's so long ago and yet I see it. Keep restoring the miracle.

▼

For next class here are some exercises: Create an old-fashioned country room with an old upright piano and music sheets from the 1900's, a sewing basket, a rocking chair, a mother, an old family album. Reminisce about the life then, recalling how you were dressed, what you did, who played the piano, how you helped your mother.

Create a garret and reminisce about going up the creaky stairs and seeing the spider webs and the old trunk. Reminisce about the objects in the trunk: the broken old doll, the picture of yourself in a party dress in 1900.

Practice reminiscing and breaking away from the action and going back to it.

BUILDING A VOCABULARY OF ACTIONS

You have come here to learn how to act, and I keep telling you I want to teach you how *not* to act — except in the very precise sense of performing actions.

What the actor is called upon to do on the stage is as broad and as limitless as life itself, and the range of actions he should have at his command is a very wide one.

The student of acting must begin to acquire a vocabulary of actions. We've already looked at "to talk," "to chat," "to converse," "to discuss," "to argue," "to fight." We've examined what it means to reminisce.

There are many actions worth studying — to take care of, to learn, to teach, to study, to reveal, to confess, to arouse, to denounce, to grieve, to wait, to be restless, to be distracted, to be shocked, to pray, to buy and sell, to advise. These are among the more important and frequently used actions, but there are, of course, many, many more.

Each takes place in specific circumstances, and each — with the exception of the actions to reminisce, to reveal oneself and to dream — requires the actor to work with a partner. The circumstances and the partner keep the action from ever becoming an abstraction. We talked about actions that are weak and that are strong — the circumstances and the partner can play an important part in making the action strong.

▼

Let's take the action "to take care of." If the object of the action to take care of is, say, a little cactus, the action is very weak, since a cactus requires almost no care at all. But if the action is to take care of a sick friend, the action becomes much stronger and much more interesting.

The nature of the action also changes according to who is performing it. If the person doing the action is a doctor it's a different action from that of an elderly immigrant or a child.

Let's try an exercise. Imagine a baby bird has fallen from a nest high in a tree. The bird is lying there helplessly, as if one wing were about to come off. The baby bird is going to die. How would you take care of it?

Who wants to go on the stage and try? Very good.

Everyone is bending to the floor. Everyone is picking up the bird very gingerly, but can you see what Brad is doing? He took the trouble to spread a handkerchief on the ground to help him pick up the injured bird. Almost all of you seem completely absorbed in the task. Seth, your gestures seem perfunctory. Have you never cared for an injured animal?

Sarah, go up on the stage and create a small play of caring for an animal.

SARAH: When I was little I had a pet turtle. Her name was Gretel and I used to like to put her in the garden. I would put out water for Gretel to swim in and lettuce leaves for her to eat. One day the small boy who lived next door made off with her, and I was afraid I would never see her again. But Gretel found her way back to the garden and I was overjoyed.

STELLA: Excellent, Sarah. You gave us a play that explained what it means to take care of an animal. In taking care of the turtle you found she had a life of her own. You also showed us there are no small stories. Only the actor makes them small.

Several times I heard Pablo Casals play. The difference between him and you is that he knows that nothing is small. No note is less important than any other note.

So far we have looked at the action to take care of on a simple human level. If you were to perform the action at a professional level — as a doctor or a nurse — you would have to visit a hospital to observe the care and you would have to practice what you have seen until it becomes second nature to you.

At the same time you have to look for the human conflict. In modern medical practice, the hospital, the patient and the doctor are all mechanized. We have eliminated the heart, and we care only mechanically. Your action of taking care of a patient will stimulate a counter-action in the patient: "Oh, forget it, you can't fool me, I'm not going to get well."

To put the counter-action into actions instead of words, the actor playing the patient would cry or hide or do something to tell us the patient was suffering from loneliness and fear and isolation. Isn't it a better play if the doctor goes out cheerfully and the patient breaks down in tears?

What does that tell us? It says there's a conflict between the mechanization of the hospital and the human heart. As actors, we must look for the human conflict, because if you play the text without interpretation nothing will happen. And the patient dies.

I once asked a student how she would play the action of taking care if the patient were an actress.

"I would take her all the telegrams and notes she has received in her dressing room," the student said.

"That's too much," I said. "It's too big. Measure is the most important thing you do on the stage. You have to measure how much time you can take to do something on stage before it becomes boring. You mustn't bring on stage a lot of things you don't care about."

You don't need to do that much on the stage. Mr. Stanislavski said it very well. He said, "Throw out 99 percent and you still have 100 per cent too much for the theatre."

That's why we have to study these actions, so we understand how to convey their essence. To take care of someone you have to be warmed inside, genuinely caring of the patient. The ingredient of caring is your talent. Many students leave that out completely. They are as clinical and mechanical as doctors.

▼

Let's look at the action "to teach." This action is related to the action "to explain." But it is far more consequential. To explain is simply to clarify something to another person. It is factual and down-to-earth.

The anatomy of "to teach" is that I give you what I know and what you *need* to know. In order to teach you something I must know something, although as an actor it may be as far from my experience as how to use a machine gun or how to cut a diamond. If those activities are not known to you either from personal experience or direct observation you must put them through your imagination.

A very useful exercise in learning the action "to teach" is to instruct the class how to make penicillin. I assume none of you are scientists, but you understand the principle of how penicillin was discovered. It was a mold, an ordinary mold that has curative properties. Peasants have known about such molds for centuries, but scientists only came to understand the properties of penicillin in the years between the two world wars.

Who would like to try to teach us how to make penicillin? All right, Gordon.

> GORDON: I'm going to teach you how to make penicillin. You can start with bread . . .
>
> STELLA: I have to interrupt you. I'm sorry, but you're making it pedestrian. You're making it pizzi-caca. You're reducing it to the level of, "How do you make ice cream?" You're pulling it down.

You're not listening to what the reason is for students coming to you to learn how to make penicillin. What makes it as important as Einstein's theory? What is it that will not pull it down to an average level?

You have to listen with your soul! Don't listen with your behind!

As a teacher you have to make direct contact with your partner. Your attachment to his soul through teaching is missing. If your action is to teach how to make penicillin you must make us realize the point is to save humanity. It must be as large as that! Is that clear?

You're not on a dramatic level. You're on a supermarket level. You have to make this important to you. Maybe you're teaching them how to make penicillin so that it could be sent to Africa. Maybe it could be sent to one of those destitute, terrible countries where not one child survives, where the children are eaten.

You must make this action important to you. If it's difficult, you must ask yourself whether you have any importance in your soul. What matters to you, beyond marriage . . . or wanting to be famous?

When you started you began with the passive action to tell

us what you were going to do. To teach is not to tell the students how we feel about the world. It's not about attitude. There's no prelude, no introduction. The impulse to teach how to make penicillin starts with your experiments.

It helps if you create circumstances for yourself, if you see the classroom full of students — there's no place for them to sit down because the room is full of laboratory equipment. This creates an air of expectation and tension that should feed the urgency of your address.

You start with the action. Acting is an extremely disciplined art. It doesn't start with, "I'm here to tell you about this play." It starts with acting. When the curtain goes up, you don't tell the audience you're going to do a scene by Tennessee Williams. You start the scene.

In an action you must know *what* you do, *where* you do it, *when* you do it, and *why* you do it. But you don't know how you do it. The how is spontaneous and unexpected.

An action can be broken up into steps or "beats." (The expression beats, by the way, isn't a musical reference. We began calling steps "beats" because members of the Moscow Art Theatre, in discussing their techniques with American actors some years ago, couldn't pronounce "bits.")

▼

We're going to work on an exercise to help us understand the action "to escape."

A revolution has broken out in a Latin American country. One village with a children's hospital has been overtaken. Outside the hospital gunfire blares. Some American Peace Corps workers on the hospital staff must evacuate and cross the border to get badly needed medical supplies from American Red Cross personnel.

To do this they must pass through enemy fire. The terrain is difficult and dangerous. A swamp, infested with deadly snakes, must be crossed. Ahead are barbed-wire barricades. The undergrowth is thick. The Peace Corps workers will brave intense cross-fire.

Left behind in the hospital lying wretchedly on their mats, the children are without food and water. Some need blood transfusions, others oxygen tents. The Peace Corps workers are carrying a vital medical prescription which must be brought out safely to the Red Cross authorities. The lives of the children depend on it.

To escape the cross-fire, the workers find temporary shelter in a mud hut. One of them takes the medical prescription out of his pocket and attempts to read it in the murky dampness of the hut. The crumpled prescription is muddied and blurred and difficult to decipher.

Searching a clearing in No Man's Land, one of the Peace Corps workers spots a Red Cross helicopter overhead and frantically signals to attract its attention. In the midst of this action a shot is fired, and the worker, wounded, falls to the ground and dies.

This exercise, which involves a pair of actors in a scene without dialogue, lasts perhaps two minutes. It illustrates the action "to escape." Within this action are a number of other actions, the sum coming under the umbrella of an overall action — to save the children.

The purpose of the exercise is to work in difficult and changing circumstances, to react to outside forces from moment to moment. While the overall action is to save the children, the immediate aim, and therefore the first of a series of actions, is to get across the border to summon help.

As an actor, you need to agitate the circumstances to feed your action. In this case the circumstances are quite agitated by themselves. The children are in danger from enemy gunfire as well as from illness. They won't survive if the medicine doesn't reach them. Escape through the swamp is made dangerous by the snakes and the crossfire. Barbed wire and landmines lie ahead.

The second action is to decipher the prescription. But the paper is so soggy and mud-stained it's no longer legible. In your mind you go back over the instructions. Your action is to try to commit them to memory. The third action is to communicate with the helicopter flying overhead by waving the American flag. The fourth action is to fall to the ground and die from the shot fired as you expose yourself signaling.

As an action, "to escape" is to run away from a troubling thought or image, or to run away from danger, but wherever you run you see the danger, take it in and run away from it, like confronting your own image in a chamber of mirrors again and again and never finding an exit. Going from danger to danger is the action "to escape." It's the action of Hamlet, Ophelia and Macbeth. The dramatic anatomy of escape is there's no escape.

This exercise reinforces our sense that as actors our primary job is to *do*, and the doing comes ahead of the words, or else the words will be false.

The action embraces a number of other actions — getting across the border, deciphering the prescription, signaling for help — but escaping is what you are doing most. What you do most is your action.

An action must have a specific end: in this case, to summon help. The end of the action determines the action and makes it strong or weak.

An action is complicated, in this case by the difficult terrain, the enemy gunfire, the barricades.

An action must be truthfully done so that we may believe in it continuously as it moves through changing circumstances.

An action must have the possibility of a partner, which can be an object such as the helicopter or a person such as the children who require help.

An action must be justified. I escape to find medical assistance for the ill and dying children.

An action must have a level or mood, a light or dark or medium level — in this case, obviously dark.

An action must have an epic meaning: A man will give his life in order to save the lives of children.

▼

Work in pairs on this exercise. Backstage, before any action begins, make a strong preparation. Visualize all the settings. Your main action is to help the children in the surrounded hospital. Uppermost in your minds should be the awareness that the children won't survive unless help reaches them. The stronger your imaginative work on the children themselves, the stronger will be all your succeeding actions.

After I give a series of raps on the table to signify gunfire, the door at the rear of the stage opens and the two actors, flat on their stomachs, work their way onto the stage, one after the other. At another series of raps, keeping low under the gunfire, they will drag themselves along the stage.

At each point the actor must justify the terrain he travels through. Across the raised stage, moving onto the studio floor, you enter the swamp, pass the barbed-wire barricade, cross No Man's Land and reach the clearing, aware all the time of the hidden dangers — the snakes, the landmines, and the enemy gunfire that at any moment may rake the ground.

In the clearing one of you removes the crumpled prescription list from his pocket and attempts to make sense of it. He sights the helicopter and begins signaling for help, exposing himself to gunfire. In his mind is one overriding thought — the children in the hospital lying helpless on their mats, locked up and gasping for breath.

Don't lose your purpose. Your purpose is to risk your life for the children. What is the idea of the playwright? That man has a duty bigger than himself. Raise it so you understand it. As an actor, you can understand this sort of commitment. You can relate it to your own sense of responsibility about your work.

"Would you be late for a performance? You have in you something of what the Peace Corps worker has, a commitment to duty."

In every case the actor has to take the play inside himself. It's not somebody else's play. It's your play. One technique for making it your play is to see how the plot and the ideas relate to you. "I will not fail my duty," you say, for you know that every man, at some point in his life, will be called upon.

I give one loud rap on the tabletop. The actor, shot in the stomach, doubles in pain, falls to the ground and dies. Each actor must find the shock to show the pain.

To do so you must use the "as if" substitution. There are, after all, certain actions we haven't experienced and aren't likely to have seen. Dying is one of them. Severe pain may be another. In the case of a severe headache we use an "as if" — we respond as if someone is punching our head or trying to bore through our forehead with an electric screwdriver. The grislier the image the better. One "as if" that's useful for dying is to imagine your guts are pouring out and we're trying to push them back inside. Eventually you're too weakened and just collapse.

The actions in this scene come swiftly, one on top of the other, but the actor must find time to criticize himself. Where was he right, and where wrong? Take enough time to decipher the prescription or part of the scene will remained unfulfilled.

One of my students got so caught up in his attempts to capture the attention of the circling helicopter that he ignored my stage signals. No matter how I tried to get his attention he kept jumping and waving, stopping the drama and spoiling the progression. An actor must correct himself as he goes along and not let emotion distort or interfere with the action.

When you've completed this exercise, even if there's still

much to correct, you will be in control of a play with a plot and can confidently say, "If I were in this situation, I could play this."

▼

You're beginning to understand how much is up to you as actors to make the play truthful. For the first time in class, you experience your own talent at work. I feel the need to warn you, "Once you feel your talent working, there is a good side and a bad side. The good side is the pleasure of knowing your talent. The bad side is that this knowledge will be the big experience of your lives and you'll never be satisfied with anything else."

Go over in your imagination the entire escape scene, from the makeshift hospital, the South American village and all the terrain to be negotiated.

Create the hut imaginatively. Where does the light come from? How high is the hut? How much space is in it? Can you stand up in it?

Establish the moment-by-moment truth from the clearing in the jungle to the dying sequence.

Practice escaping from a room filled with gas, from a house on fire, from a gang of kids who are attacking you, from jail.

Keep in mind that the anatomy of the action "to escape" is that you have no place to go. Beyond the swamp is the barbed wire, beyond the barbed wire No Man's Land. What you are trying to escape from is not escapable. If you're bound to a chair, and escaping from it is a matter of life and death, you don't succeed. The cockroach you chase doesn't get away. Wherever you turn in search of a way out, a bigger obstacle awaits.

INSTANT AND INNER JUSTIFICATIONS

When we act, primarily we perform an action. Our second objective is creating a reason for the action. This is called justification, and before we continue examining actions we must look into it.

The justification isn't in the lines, but in you. What you choose as your justification should agitate you, should help you experience the action and the emotion. If you experience nothing, you've made a dead choice. It doesn't warm you. It doesn't agitate you. You have to choose something that will awaken you.

Your talent consists in how well you "shop" for your justification. Your justification is what gives size to your actions. You must make every action you perform epic.

Working in that way makes you grow. You grow through acting more than through living. The ideas you get from plays will make you bigger.

Justification goes on continuously in the mind of the actor for as long as he's on stage. Finding reasons for everything you do on the stage keeps your actions truthful. The creative part of your work, justification, is what you live on in the theatre.

There are two kinds of justification, instant and inner.

Instant justification gives you the immediate reason for what you're doing. It removes the abstract part of acting. If I love you, what do I do? I sing with you, I dance with you. I put your coat on for you. I give you a flower.

Physicalizing the emotions is essential in the theatre, and the more detailed the physicalization or justification, the better. If you've introduced a basket into the stage action, we want to know how heavy the basket is, what's inside, who it belongs to, why it was on the shelf.

Why are you opening the window? To get some fresh air is an example of instant justification. To see what made that sudden crashing noise is another. Why are you closing the window? So the flies don't come in is one instant justification. To stop the breeze from rattling the shades is another.

Instant justification supplies the immediate need. It answers the why in our series of who, what, where, when and why questions.

Why did you close the dressing room door? I was changing my clothes. The hinge was squeaking. I needed the props that were holding it open. To surprise people with my new costume. To keep out the rehearsal music. All of these are spontaneous justifications for the action of closing the door. They're not profound, but they're plausible.

With instant justification you can't be too elaborate. You can't say I closed the door because there was an actor in the hall I didn't want to see. This is an example of what we call adding fiction to fiction. A person we can't possibly know anything about has been brought needlessly into the picture. When you do that instant justification goes out the window.

Who can give me three reasons why you want a glass of water?

JENNIFER: I need to take some vitamins.

STELLA: Good.

ANNE: I want to gargle.

STELLA: Good.

ROBERT: I'm thirsty.

STELLA: I know that sounds obvious, but it's not good. Why is "I'm thirsty" not a good justification? Because it's too subjective. It's a state of being. You need to find a justification that you can do. "I need water as a chaser for my drink." "I need water to wipe a spot off my dress." "I need water to take an aspirin."

Avoid subjective reasons when you're making an instant justification. Why am I rapping on the table? I'm going to give you several justifications. You tell me which one is not acceptable. To try to get attention. To kill a cockroach. Because I'm angry.

That wasn't hard, was it? To say you're angry is to make something up inside yourself. You can't go to the emotions for instant justification. You must go to the immediate circumstances, to something readily doable,

Why are you opening the desk drawer? To get a pencil. To take out my keys. To get stamps for a letter. To see if the handle has been repaired. Each justification must have a logic that will enable you to extend the logic. To get a pencil and some stationery to write a letter. To take out my keys so I can lock the desk and leave.

Justification must go on all the time in even the most mundane actions of daily life. It is your prime source of awakening to doing and to feeling.

Let's imagine that in the space in front of us is a garden with trees and a pool. Imagine three things you can do in this space, and create a reason for each. Practicing instant justification, you must deal only with what's directly in front of you.

"I'm going to climb a tree." This statement, describing an action without a stated purpose, is not enough. It does not provide the why. "I'm going to climb a tree to pick an apple." Now we have the justification.

Sometimes students are tempted to expand on the reason by adding, "I'm going to climb the tree to pick some apples to give to my friends." The friends have been brought in unnecessarily. They don't belong there. They're adding fiction to fiction.

For the purpose of instant justification you must deal only with what's directly in front of you. You can say, "I want to climb the tree to get a nice juicy apple that is good to eat." Now the apple begins to take on the life of the place. To say you want to give some apples to your friends is simply fake plotting.

Try some other actions in this garden by the pool. Why do you put your hand in the water? Quite simply, to test it. By continuing with this logic, you discover what else you can do in these circumstances. Why did you wipe your hand? The simplest answer is, Because it's wet. A little more complicated but acceptable is, Because the water's slimy.

Why are you reaching down with your right hand? Not to get a match, which you don't need and which again is outside the logic of this setting. Instead, reach down for something you need when you lie in the sun, such as sunglasses or suntan lotion. Continue with the logic of the circumstances.

There's no need to make the action more elaborate. For example, you don't move under the tree to "escape the glare of the pool." That's too fancy — another example of adding fakeness to the action, and it's not instant justification.

You take your sweater off because you're hot, not to make yourself "feel comfortable." You can't say, "I feel terribly warm." It's better to say, "My blouse is sticking to me. I must go and change it and take a bath." Steer away from such words as comfortable, convenient, glaring and beautiful, because they take you too far away from the impulse activity.

If you talk too much, you're not doing it, and if you don't do it you are not finding the instant justification for your action.

Justifications can be logical, common, or they can be creative and uncommon. For instance, an uncommon justification for helping someone on the street is he's blind and no one else bothered to assist him.

Full and unqualified belief in the answer you give is always implied in your choice of the justification. Each justification must pass through your imagination so that it becomes more personal and individual and thereby more interesting and vivid to the audience.

Why are you reading the book? Because it's on anthropology, which I'm studying. A better reason is, Because it explains the technique of acting, which I'm studying. Why are you fixing the chair? Because it's an antique, and I can give it to the museum.

Why are you taking off your shoe? You can say, Because it's tight, but a more interesting answer would be, Because I need to get the circulation going in my arthritic toes.

You must choose justifications to which you react immediately. You must believe what you are say. Through justifications the actor has a real place in the theatre because he is giving life to the lines. If the actor hasn't used his imagination he's made no contribution.

Justification must have a level — light, dark or medium. Justification on a dark level occurs when you describe a winter scene on the Bowery or an avalanche in the Alps. These imply menace. You can agitate them even further by adding details — after the avalanche you have to warm the bodies with towels and blankets; you have to make a path through the fallen trees and brush to reach the hospital.

The addition of agitating details affects the actor's emotions. The levels go with the circumstances. The doing of actions, backed up by instant justification, relieves the actor of the unreasonable pressure to resort to amorphous and unreliable feelings. People don't act. They experience something. They experience one moment, then the next moment, then the next moment. The justification is your talent; don't go where your talent can't possibly follow.

I'd like one of you to go and sit on the edge of the stage. Thank you.

> STELLA: Andrew, why are you sitting on the edge of the stage?
>
> ANDREW: I'm sitting because I want to get a better perspective of the stage.
>
> STELLA: Cut out that phony college word *perspective* and say instead, quite simply, "I am sitting here because I want to see the stage."

When you say, "I want to get a better perspective of the stage," you have not used words that enliven you. Avoid words that don't warm you. When you see something, you must make me see it too. I won't if your choice of words is cold and remote.

The physical, doable side of acting is what matters. If you read something in the newspaper that you like, tear it out. The action tells us something.

If an actor fails to protect himself onstage by physicalizing his actions, we're likely to catch him "acting," playing a mood. Instead of protecting himself by picking up a letter, or putting the keys away, or seeing that the lights are on, we've caught him attempting to act feelings. The mood of the play will be there, but not the life of the play. On stage, when life comes in, we should forever celebrate it.

▼

Always, always keep yourself out of it. Say to yourself: I myself don't count. The world counts. If I am beautiful, it's not my beauty that's important in my actions. It's not the beautiful and suffering side of myself that counts, but what I do.

In life, as on the stage, it's not who I *am* but what I *do* that's the measure of my worth and the secret of my success. All the rest is showiness, arrogance and conceit.

I'm going to ask you a question and I want someone to give me an instant justification. Why do you complain about going out in the morning?

JANE: Because the elevator takes ten minutes to get to the seventh floor, and I hate to walk down seven flights before I reach the street.

STELLA: Good, Jane. This justification is strong and correct, but it also presents a danger.

The moment you use the first person singular or words like "love" or "hate," which have high emotional content, the justification demands are stronger. You have to pay a price for using the "I." You've raised the stakes to a greater investment in your justification.

All right, I have another question and I'd like several of you to give me instant justifications. Why did Brad help the person across the street?

JENNIFER: Brad likes helping people.

STELLA: Unless the justification is strong, it is best to avoid words like helping, feeling, loving, caring. It is better to use the circumstances, the place and what you actually see. You cannot see, He liked helping people. Rather we want to know what he did.

Let's have another justification.

ANDREW: There was nobody else around.

STELLA: That's not much help either.

ANNE: He helped the person across the street because he was thinking about his mother.

ROBERT: He helped the lady across the street because she had invited him to a party.

STELLA: All these answers were nothing but fake plots, assumptions of a past history that could not be known. They're all evasions of the need to be concrete and to visualize the action. Why are you evading what you could control and choosing what you couldn't? Your answers were journalistic and false. Instead, a more useful answer would have been, "He helped the man across the street because he saw that he was old and limping and laboring under heavy packages."

Why are you setting the table? If I say, "Because my boyfriend is coming," I have weakened the action and the justification. It has none of the excitement of, "The doorbell's ringing and the table isn't set." Or, "The telephone's ringing, and I know it's my mother and I'll have to tell her I didn't set the table yet." The phone ringing excites me to action.

In each case the circumstances are lively and immediate, contributing spontaneous justification for my action of setting the table.

STELLA: Andrew, why are you turning off the lights?

ANDREW: Because I am tired.

STELLA: That's a fake answer. Try again.

ANDREW: It's my girlfriend's surprise party.

STELLA: That's better, but it can be more exciting: "Let's have it dark. Not a light in the room. It's a surprise party."

In other words, make it doable. But don't go where your talent can't follow. How many of you play an instrument. (*A number of students raise their hands.*)

Then you know that an instrument has a scale: C, D, E, F. Why did you want to play an instrument without a scale? If you don't know half-tones or the 12-tone row, why do you insist on trying to play them?

▼

Instant justification is what gets the motor started. To keep it running you have to have inner justification. Instant justification doesn't affect me inside. Inner justification does. It arouses and moves me. Inner justification is what the actor contributes to the playwright's lines.

Relating to what lies behind the text, inner justification has less to do with the object, more to do with why the object is used in a certain way or why the action is done in a certain way.

The "why" is personal to the actor and belongs to him. The author gives you the outlines but you as the actor must write the play. When I say to a person, "You ought to stop rushing," what I'm really saying is, "You're too anxious."

A scene takes place in a hospital corridor. The script has the doctor asking the nurse, "Did you give him the medicine?" She answers, "No," but her answer has more force than the matter-of-fact word because her inner justification is that the patient has stopped breathing.

In a restaurant a man asks a woman if she'd like some sugar. She says, "No, thank you." Her answer has great strength because her inner justification is that she has diabetes.

In class I can turn to my assistant Pearl, who is wearing a black dress like mine. I say to her, "Please don't wear black." This is the only line. What I'm really saying, my inner monologue, is, "I don't want the students to see teachers always dressed in black because it's depressing."

I don't give Pearl this inner reason, but it lies behind the words and it must be understood by the audience to lie behind the words. I can say to one of you, "I don't want you to wear any more pleated skirts." What I'am really saying is that she should get used to different styles of clothing if she wants to be an actress.

Or I can say, "It would be better if you wore your hair in braids." Inside, my inner justification is, "If you wore your hair in braids, it will remind you of the style of another period, which, in turn, will give you the needed quiet for playing this part."

If I were to say, "Jennifer, I don't want you to take any more notes," my meaning is, "You're putting all your attention into your writing and neglecting the class teaching. This is a school-girl habit, and I want you to stop."

The author doesn't give you the actor's contribution. The monologue of the actor is the inner justification. The actor's justification is a continuing process. What goes on within you and what you actually say are, of course, different. To a student I might say, "How are you? It's nice you don't miss class." Inside I'm saying, "He's so ambitious. He's always raising his hand. I find him boring."

One has to keep justifying all the time. In justifying one's relationship to the partner, to the circumstances of the scene and to the props, the motor must never stop. If justification stops, one goes dead inside, and dead pockets will result on stage.

I may say to an actor, "I want to talk to you sometime." That's all I say, but the inner monologue goes as follows: I see you have the habit of being a loner. This isolates you, puts icicles around you. I want to break down those icicles.

There's no limit to how deep inner justification can go. Anne, go up on stage.

STELLA: Do you have any pictures of your family?

ANNE: Yes.

STELLA: Do you think of yourself as being very modern?

ANNE: No, I don't at all.

STELLA: Have I talked to you very much?

ANNE: Not personally.

STELLA: All right, let me tell you what I was thinking. I asked the first question because you seemed to have a feeling for traditional clothes. You've been influenced by another generation. What I was thinking when I asked the second question was that you looked like an old-fashioned painting. It wasn't entirely a compliment because I thought you were mixing yourself up by wearing sweaters of another generation. As you can see, I was getting deeper. For the last question I thought, "You're really not lending yourself to being an actor. You haven't joined the mob yet. You behave like a visitor. You don't make contact as an actor. That's why I haven't talked to you."

The answers to these questions must also be given inner justification. If you answer them straightforwardly, factually, you'll be a boring actress.

The answer to the question, "Do you live at home?" can be given in different ways and with different tones and shades of meaning. The successful actress is the one who, in giving her answer, experiences what made her not live at home. By her answer she can intimate why she left.

What you awaken in yourself is your contribution to the words. You can't simply repeat facts, adding nothing. Justification turns facts into experience. Each person justifies according to his talent, and the justification *is* his talent.

If you don't justify your actions, you'll be caught acting. In Shakespeare every line tells you what to do. In modern plays it's left to you and it will be hollow unless you have adequate instant and inner justification.

You must not be caught acting in the modern theatre because the audience expects to see someone who looks and behaves as they do, or their aunt, or their cousin. Nobody in the theatre before 1860 looked like you. Or spoke like you. They spoke verse and were so aristocratic or upper middle class in appearance that they'd be easily distinguishable from you.

You belong to the democratic world that came after 1860. You need an aesthetic and a style of such plainness that your appearance and your voice won't take on any artificiality. If you stop acting and instead do something, the doing will absorb the fake. In your justification of what you're doing, you avoid indicating, and in the modern style of acting, above all, you must not indicate.

▼

Here are some exercises to help you understand justification: Give me five reasons why you complimented somebody, why you left your job, why you helped someone on the street, why the man crossed the street so fast, why the mother left the package at the department store.

Give five reasons why you opened the window, why you closed the window.

Trace what you do in circumstances when you feel these emotions: I'm so happy, I'm so angry, I'm so pleased.

Justify on a dark level in ten different ways the line, "He'll be glad about that."

Give ten inner justifications for reading a book, getting dressed, going downtown.

Give five reasons for complaining in the theatre, in a story, on the subway.

A woman enters a grocery story. Imagine what she will buy and why.

Be prepared to answer the following questions about a basket: What kind is it? How heavy is it? What's inside it? Whose is it? Why is it on the shelf?

Strike a pose. Relax every muscle except those needed for the pose. Justify the pose. Example: You raise your hand. Why? To fix the washing on the line. Or, to prevent the basket from falling.

Take four poses, justify each and link them together in the justification. Example: (1) Raise your right hand. (2) Put your hand to your forehead. (3) Put your left hand in your pocket. The justifications are (1) to hush the audience, (2) to recall the speech, and (3) to search for your notes.

Lastly, here are a few lines. Break up into pairs and perform them for us. They don't make much sense on the surface. It's your job to give them an inner justification. Make them logical and compelling.

"I wouldn't go in there if I were you."
"How long has she been like that?"
"Her dress still has the stains on it."
"Has he left yet?"
"I heard a door slam hours ago."
"But I'm sure the blue car is his."

COMPLICATING ACTIONS

It's not enough to study actions. It's not enough to understand them. You must master them. Make them absolutely your own. It's a preparation for when we approach dramatic texts. We'll have to master them too. We'll have to master the authors.

God help us if Toscanini had gotten up and said, "I wonder what Beethoven meant." Toscanini said, "Come on now, Beethoven. I've got you."

You are in control. You are never out of control. You're the master. You own the thing. "Come on, Shakespeare," you must be able to say. "Shakespeare, come on, let's go."

But you're so frightened you have no control. That's why you have to spend your time studying, rehearsing, so that when you come to class you can say to yourself, "I own that. She's not going to tell me anything new about that."

You have to come to class as the boss. Don't come to me. I'm not Mama. In a sense I'm not a teacher. I watched horses this summer. I saw people who were learning to ride. The horses know what to do. The horses have been taught how to respond to commands. You should have seen the riders practicing the jumps. The teacher wasn't there. They had to know how to control the horse, or break their necks.

You're on that horse alone in this class. I can only give you so much. You must put the work in. Nobody's going to carry you.

What you must have seen by now is there are no mysteries to what we do. There is logic. You're always working with a partner. You're always in circumstances. Understanding your relationship with your partner, whether it's another actor or the audience, and the proper building of circumstances are the keys to what you must do on stage.

You don't hear me talk much about emotions. That's because emotions aren't doable. Actions are doable, and if you do them correctly, they prompt the feelings.

When I worked with Stanislavski in Paris he stressed the importance of the imagination. He explained how important it was to use the imagination on the stage. He explained in detail how important it was to use the circumstances. He said that *where* you are is what you are and how you are and what you can be. You are in a place that will feed you, that will give you strength, that will give you the ability to do whatever you want.

All the emotion required of you can be found through your imagination and in the circumstances of the play. You must understand that you can only exist truthfully on stage when you're in those circumstances.

If you need an action you can't find in a play then you can go back to your own life — but not for the emotion, rather for a similar action. In your own personal experience you had a similar action to which you had an emotional response. Go back to the action and the specific circumstances and remember what you did. If you recall the place, the feelings will come back to you.

But to remain in your personal past, which made you cry or gave you a past emotion, is false, because you're not now in those circumstances. You're in the play, and it's the play's circumstances that have to be done truthfully by borrowing what was physical from the past action, not the emotion. You cannot stitch together a character from how you felt when your pet rabbit died or that time you visited your terminally ill grandmother in the hospital.

Your work doesn't begin when you arrive on stage. It begins in the wings. When you make an entrance it must never be simply because your cue has come. Whenever you enter or leave the stage, you go into circumstances. That means you have come from somewhere and you're going someplace. A good actor doesn't enter from the wings. Before he enters he makes a preparation. He's found a need to walk on that has nothing to do with the stage manager's cues.

You must prepare for every entrance by creating the circumstances of where you've come from. This need not be elaborate. All it should require is a tiny detail that makes that place real for you.

You must also justify every entrance. There must be a reason why you have entered the circumstances of the play. To do this in fact, and not simply have the justification in your head, you must physicalize the action of entering. Pick up the mail while coming in, not after coming in. Put change in your pocketbook while coming in. Never start with the beginning of something. The curtain goes up while you are in the middle or at the end of doing something.

It's best if you can find a prop to give you a sense of the reality. On the stage whatever you do that's physical does not lie. Harold Clurman wrote a book about the theatre and called it *Lies Like Truth*. The lie has to become the truth in your hands. That's your job as an actor — it is the highest responsibility you have — to erase the lie of the dramatic plot.

The great paradox of acting is that the actor must act real things in an unreal, imaginary setting. You must do everything you can to make the world of the stage real, and you do that by actions. If you go to your memories you're creating your own play, not the author's.

Stanislavski said that one can demand of an actor that he *do* something. You can never demand of him that he *feel* something. The reason you must have a vocabulary of actions is so that you can go directly to them, not to your little life in Brooklyn.

If I were to illustrate entering a classroom to teach a class in acting I might take off my coat as I enter, remove my gloves and arrange notebooks on the table for the day's work. I might put up my hair for the class. I'd start the activity off stage so that I finish as I enter. The taking off of a coat and gloves illustrate where I've come from.

If you start an action outside, such as taking off your coat, and continue it as you move onto the stage it will give you the sense of not coming in. You'll have come from somewhere, and the action in itself will have reduced the tension of making an entrance.

Don't come on singing like an overly cheerful nurse bringing a tray to a hospital patient. "De dum, de dum, have I got something nice for you." Singing is making an entrance. It has nothing to do with psychological acting.

You must be able to go off and come back so that we know life has continued, or be able to go to another room and return with some element of change. Enter a room after you've already done four things so the audience knows what you were doing. When you come into an office from the corridor, enter doing something — with a bill to pay or a book to return.

If you enter with fresh-cut flowers and put them into a vase the audience can infer you've come from the garden. The preparation will keep you from tightening up. The prop will keep you truthful.

Choose something doable, not show-able. None of this is for the sake of the audience. It's for *your* sake. You must be so thoroughly involved you'll sense if you're overdoing it.

These are very basic actions. The ones that matter are those that make demands on our imaginations. If I say I'd like you now to draw a pumpkin on your hand you have an action. You have to begin by saying, "What will I draw with? With a yellow crayon." You must have this sense of truth Is this clear to you? The drawing must be something you control.

▼

Let's try something a little bigger. I'd like you to hold a palette, hold a brush, and in front of you see a little canvas on which you'll paint a daisy.

See the color of the canvas? Begin to say, "Do I know how to hold the brush? What's the nature of the brush?" Immediately I do this. Then I know if I really can hold the brush. Then I'm going to wash the brush, put it in the white paint and follow my action. I'm going to draw. Now, before I draw I already see my canvas is outlined in pencil. In this way I make the canvas mine, make the brush mine. I don't just say, "Here's the brush and I'll paint the daisy."

I say my brush is dirty. (That makes it mine.) Now I'm ready to use the paint. Every physical action is much better if it's yours, if it bears your signature. You must reach your norm, not my norm. You must make everything belong to you — your brush, your canvas, your daisy.

Start with these physical actions truthfully. Also justify why you are painting the daisy. Because the little girl for whom you are babysitting asked you to or because you want to find out if this new German paint is any good. But first you have to ask, "Can I paint a daisy?" Then reinforce it with other things.

Once you understand the basic elements of an action you have to complicate them. Let's say my action is to sew. To sew what? To sew the fabric together. To make the action belong to you you have to know the fabric. If I say, "I'm going to sew this miserable, dirty, horrible sock," then I know it. It's mine. Make the action yours. Don't put it in the world of demonstration, of showing.

From now on never take the simplest road. Who understands what I mean? For even the simplest action find something to complicate it. On the one hand it's good for the audience because it's not boring. But it's even better for you, because the more little tasks you give yourself within the action the more you have to concentrate on, the less likely you are to indicate.

▼

Let's take the action to comb the hair. This is a pretty straightforward action. How can we complicate it? You want me to tease my hair. Good idea. That makes it more complicated, more interesting, a little more difficult. To comb my hair with a hairnet on. Good. It means I must first take my hairnet off. To comb my hair with curlers. Good. I have to remove the curlers. I have flowers in my hair. Wonderful! That means I have to comb around them.

How can you complicate putting your shoes on? Well, the laces can be tied in knots. Or the shoes have shoe trees in them. Or the shoes are wet. Or the laces are broken. Or you see the shoes have a stain and need to be polished. All of these give the simple action some interesting complications.

Complicating the action doesn't mean that you throw all logic and good sense aside. Some years ago in class I set out six chairs and told the students to sit in them. Six students came forward and sat down. I asked them to get up. I then placed some books on each chair. "Now I've complicated your action," I said. The same six actors went to the chairs and sat on top of the books.

Next, I spilled a little coffee on each chair and told them to sit again. Five of the actors dutifully marched to the chairs and sat down in the coffee, but the sixth held out. Instead she took a rag and wiped the chair dry before taking her place.

"Thank God!" I said.

An action isn't always made up of a large truth. It's made up of tiny little truths. If you skip one, you're shaken. You're rocked. There are always many little truths on the stage and sometimes you skip them. How do you fix them?

Sometimes on stage you're looking for something, only you are not really looking. And this frightens you. It should frighten you. If you make a little untruth of one thing, that little untruth accumulates into another little untruth and another, and by that time you've frightened the goddam hell out of yourself, and something happens. Either you do too much or too little, or you're afraid.

All actions can be complicated, and you have to get a sense of doing them truthfully. You must overcome your desire to do the whole thing instead of being very patient. If I want to take a splinter out and I take the needle and sterilize it and it's black and I don't know whether to use it because it's black, I'm working correctly.

But if I overlook these little truths and just grab a needle and say, "Ooo, I'm going to take the splinter out," I haven't done my homework. No physical action is done all together. It grows from one thing to another. If I pick the needle up, it will be black. If it's black, I'll know that maybe I have to wipe it. If I wipe it, really, and I have to get the splinter, I'll know the splinter is a little bit sticking out. As long as I work this way I'll have no problems. You're only uncomfortable if you use the lazy approach and generalize.

▼

Justifying the action complicates it and makes it stronger. We've worked on scraping imaginary mud off our shoes. If you begin to really take off the mud there's no way for you to be uncomfortable. Later on if you justify the action by imagining

STELLA ADLER — A LIFE IN THE THEATRE

TEACHING, CIRCA 1988

ABOVE, IN THE GROUP THEATRE PRODUCTION OF CLIFFORD ODETS' *AWAKE AND SING*

RIGHT, WITH JOHN ABBOTT IN *HE WHO GETS SLAPPED* AT THE

BOOTH THEATRE, 1946

IN THE 1936 PARAMOUNT FILM *LOVE ON TOAST*

ABOVE, AGAIN IN THE
1936 PARAMOUNT FILM
LOVE ON TOAST

RIGHT, IN THE 1948
UNITED ARTISTS FILM
MY GIRL TISA

LEFT, STELLA
TEACHING CIRCA 1980

BELOW, PUBLICITY
SHOT FROM THE 40'S

RIGHT, PUBLICITY
SHOT, 1935

PHOTOS COURTESY OF: IRENE GILBERT, ARCHIVAL COLLECTION, STELLA ADLER ACADEMY AND THEATRE — LOS ANGELES

IN THE STELLA ADLER THEATRE, LOS ANGELES, 1991

you've killed someone and you don't want anyone to know that you've been out in the street *and* you must do it quickly . . . you must STILL take off the mud, but you have a lot of reasons to make it more interesting.

Every action grows when you imagine it in circumstances. You need to make things belong to you. It doesn't belong to the realm of general acting. This is what's important. Through using your aliveness to it, you relax.

Take three simple physical actions in sequence and build a plot around them.

> (1) Look out the window;
> (2) Straighten the desk;
> (3) Take hat and coat and leave.

Or:

> (1) Write something in a letter;
> (2) Start to telephone;
> (3) Pick up your pocketbook and leave.

None of these is a difficult action, but they only become interesting onstage if you break them up into little actions and, more important, if you create a justification for each. Using these actions, create a play first on the light, then on the dark level.

Remember, every action consists of many little actions. If your overall action is to leave for a holiday, the action of the scene will be to pack a suitcase. Taking shorts out of the drawer and putting them in a suitcase, taking the toilet articles from the bathroom and packing them both have to do with going on a holiday. While packing you might take your checkbook out to see how much money you have, and that also would be part of the nature of taking a holiday.

Life intrudes on your steps. The telephone rings, and you have to answer it. The call might be from the accountant about your taxes. It might be about theatre tickets. These are instances of life coming in on your actions.

Still, you're in your room with your suitcase and mostly you're packing. Why? What, in other words, is the justification? To go on a holiday. You must also determine the mood of the action. Is it on a light, dark or medium level? A dark level would be leaving to visit a relative dying in a hospital. You don't reveal your feelings to the relative. You yourself know they're dark.

If you're simply going away for the weekend the level can't be dark. A weekend outing has a light connotation. Still, you can't play going away for the weekend without knowing a number of other things about the character. What does he do for a living? What's his profession? His social position? His morality? His politics? His ethics? His attitude toward family, society and sex? Every choice affects how the character approaches the weekend.

▼

Be careful to do nothing to sidestep from the action. Do everything to make it grow. Don't use props accidentally. Externalize what's going on inside of you. From your physicalizations the audience will identify with your feelings and understand the action. Make a selection of props, language and thoughts to reveal your feeling about the action and what's going on inside of you. Be selective about your gestures. By what a character does you discover most of what you need to know about him.

An exercise Stanislavski liked was to take three things in a place and build a play around them, first on the light level, then on a dark level. The three things are a birdcage, a valise and a coat. Where you put these objects will determine the lightness or the darkness. It will also affect the plot.

Never be on stage without a situation, an imaginative situation that's not your situation but the situation of the play. Your job is to fill the play with the truth.

Another useful exercise is to create justifications around the following dialogue that let you perform it first on the light level, then on the dark:

A: I told you it was dangerous.

B: It wasn't, in the beginning.

A: He must have heard something when the door opened.

B: Everybody heard it. That isn't what changed his mind.

A: What changed his mind was in the letter you read.

B: I know, and you know as well as I do what he meant.

A: Yes, I know, and I'm sorry about it.

Let me give you a very dark play plot, and see how you can develop it. I'm looking out the window over the park. My husband has left me. The pile of boots is arranged in the corner just as he left them. It was the last thing he did before going. He put on his coat. He took off his ring and left it on the table. He went out and closed the door behind him. Now he's gone forever.

First we want to see him do these things. Then we want to see you respond to the objects left. You have to know how to work physically with three or four things in a room that will make you respond to the situation called for by the imaginative plot.

GIVING ACTIONS SIZE

So far your actions have been on a fairly simple level, though I hope you see their complexity and interest depend on your imagination. Some actions, of course, are complicated to begin with. We need to understand them to do weightier plays.

The action "to grieve," for example. To grieve means to lose something forever. Something dear to you has been taken away, and you must find this experience of loss. Generally this is an action you've known or at least seen.

Another larger action is "to philosophize." To philosophize is to probe human behavior, to penetrate life's mystery. It's an intellectual game, so there should be enjoyment in it. It's like discussion, but without the fervor. You frequently find it in Shaw.

An action you'll frequently be called upon to perform is "to advise." To give advice to a person means he or she needs to know something you can explain or clarify. You advise someone about real estate, about finances, home life, their personal life. Where do you go for advice? To a doctor's office, a lawyer's office, your parents, the person next door.

The anatomy of advice projects order, fluency, spontaneity. Far from being static, advice calls for a certain rhythm that goes with the action's characteristic gesture, pointing the finger for emphasis. It's a repeated action.

"To advise" is all mind. It doesn't come from the heart but from the head. Advice, therefore, is not like teaching, which goes from my heart to yours. When you go to a policeman for advice, he doesn't "teach" you how to get to the subway. Nor does the doctor "teach" you what medicine to take. They advise you. I advise you how to find water in the desert. I tell you to follow the camel tracks, which lead to a grove, and in that grove you'll find water.

Giving advice requires logic. You must arrange your points and deliver them in order — one, two, three, four. To the prospective student of acting, your advice may be that school is bad for actors. You arrange your points: school will give you habits difficult to break and will harm your talent. Regardless of your feelings, you'll have to do what they tell you. You won't be asked to raise your talent to its highest level. School brings you down to its level.

In addition to cold, reasoned logic, advice is generally dark in mood. It has something to do with being professional. To get the necessary note of authority into the voice, an actor giving advice assures himself he knows something very important that the person receiving the advice doesn't know.

▼

A more complex action is "to confess" or "to reveal oneself." Revealing is opening up the inner self and exposing your deepest thoughts to another without holding back. It's a universal human experience, one we find often in the theatre.

Confessing is associated with strong feelings, but as in all actions, your attempt shouldn't be to express them directly, but to focus on the action and let the feelings come in response to the action. To put the action on a more mundane level, when you "reveal yourself" to your doctor by telling him your symptoms, you say, "Doctor, I can't shake like this any more. I need some medicine."

The action is to go to the doctor, to be examined, to confess everything, to reveal all your symptoms. By doing that, you hope to find relief, but the *action* is to confess, not to find relief. Your doctor will talk to you, comfort you, calm you. All that is within the action. You don't *play* the relief.

We think of going to the doctor as a fairly clinical action, cut and dried, but what the revelation of symptoms has in common with other kinds of confession is that it involves careful, rigorous self-examination and has as its object the relieving of some kind of pain.

Most often when we hear "to confess" we think of a crime. If I confess to a crime, I may do so to get a lighter punishment or to protect a falsely accused person. You mustn't say you confess your crime in order to relieve your guilt. That will come, but *the feeling must follow from the action*.

Imagine you have killed someone under difficult circumstances. There's no possible help for what you've done anymore than if you'd killed yourself. You're up against a stone wall, and you want to confess. Find something in yourself that says you can't be any different from the way you are. Nobody can help what they do. There's a killer in all of us.

To make this statement, acknowledge you've already failed yourself in major areas. You can say, "I've wasted my life and there's no taking it back." It's the experience of being trapped, a situation found in almost every modern play, a sense of helplessness and failure, the realization finally that everyone fails. Nobody is a success.

"I could have had it all," you say. "But I let it go. People spent time and money on me, but I was lazy. I didn't pay attention. It's gone now and I'll never have it back." Yes, even you, like Terry Molloy, could've been a contender.

The intention of this confession is: "I want you to know me for the first time." It's the action of Anna Christie in Eugene O'Neill's play when she confesses her past life of prostitution to

Matt, her lover, and to her father. Confession compels attention, as her speech illustrates:

> You will too listen! You — keeping me safe inland — I
> wasn't no nurse girl the last two years — I lied when I
> wrote you — I was in a house, that's what! — Yes, that
> kind of house — the kind sailors, you and Matt, goes to
> in port — and your nice inland men, too — and all men,
> God damn 'em'! I hate 'em! I hate 'em!

Confession seeks a kind of purification, which Anna believed
she'd gain through Matt's love, and by running away to the
cleansing sea, to be reunited with her lost father and reawaken
the blood memory of her true relationship to the universe.

The action is a tearing open of the truth, a pulling out of an
inner life not so clear even to oneself, a vomiting out of personal truth. It's one of the deepest human actions. In O'Neill, in
Odets, in Tennessee Williams, the lesson of their confessions is
that there's no way out.

Revelation or confession is not a manifestation of sickness or
neurosis, but consists of penetrating through darkness to some
truth, to the realization of what it is to be human. It's a biblical
statement.

Either through art or through science the whole quest of
man is to have some size — the stature required to express to the
world what you have learned about it. The whole of man is
directed to this one effort, and the whole of playwriting shows
that aim. Revealing means to take off the cover, to unmask your
soul. It's large and epic in scope.

Try confessing something that distresses you deeply, something that made you lose yourself:

"I love that man. I love his children. I can't help it. I love his
wife."

To act you must be able to make this sort of confession. If
you say where you've failed, or whom you've failed, or how you

feel about your own failure, you'll have arrived at an action that runs unceasingly through the whole of modern theatre.

▼

Acting requires a creative and compassionate attitude. It must aim to lift life up to a higher level of meaning and not tear it down or demean it. The actor's search is a generous quest for that larger meaning.

That's why acting is never to be done passively. When I watch some of you I sense you're not really involved. Some of you become totally detached from the work of other students in the class. There's an unspoken criticalness or indifference, which is disruptive to the class and hinders you from learning. It's a trait that ill serves actors. Instead of being critical and judgmental, we should recognize and honor others' efforts. Criticizing others, belittling others only diminishes us. And if our goal is always size, that's heading in the wrong direction!

▼

Another action that requires size is "to denounce." This action assumes the existence of an enemy and has in it the element of attack. To denounce is to put someone in his place, to cry him down, to destroy him. It's an action performed by someone with real power speaking from a platform or throne. From the King to his enemies or, as in *Waiting for Lefty*, from the strike leader to the bosses.

Denunciation is not a petty action. It's not "ratting" on someone. That implies pettiness and meanness. Denunciation comes from one archetype to another, an attack not on an individual but on the institution the individual represents.

To denounce is the action Coriolanus performs in his "common cry of curs" speech. With a bravery honored even by his enemies, Coriolanus won his wars and had the role of Consul thrust upon him by a grateful Rome. But he treated the masses with undisguised contempt, earning the name of tyrant and suffering eventual banishment. The decree of banishment provoked his anger:

> You common cry of curs! Whose breath I hate
> As reeks of the rotten fens, whose loves I prize
> As the dead carcasses of unburied men
> That do corrupt my air, I banish you;
> And here remain with your uncertainty!
> Let every feeble rumor shake your hearts!
> Your enemies, with nodding of their plumes,
> Fan you into despair!

The person who denounces believes nobody can touch him. Brutus says of Coriolanus, "As if you were a god to punish, not a man of their infirmity." In this speech Coriolanus is saying, "I represent what I really represent, and you don't. I will tell you what you really are." There's no pleading, no attempt to remedy the situation.

"To denounce" is difficult for young students because it requires size and physical presence and because the action itself is alien to our culture. As actors you have to find or borrow the action. Borrow an image: you are the biggest machine on the construction site, the crane, beside which everything else is insignificant.

You need to locate a sense of power in order to denounce, and it must come from inside you, must be in you before you start. Start by denouncing bankers, oil company operators, people who start wars. Suit the body to the words. The body must accompany the expression of the idea.

In your walk and posture, in how you stand, in how you gesture, you must find the necessary power and size. The power is in your gut, in your stomach. Judge how much energy or effort you need for any gesture. Have full control of yourself physically so at any moment you can make yourself a living sculpture.

▼

An action close to denunciation is "to defy." If you were to make the action of defiance with your hands, it would be a thrusting, chopping, rhythmic slashing of the air, a striking out. The action of defiance is to cut down a man, to demolish his ideas as utterly as you'd chop a tree to the ground. It is an action requiring the stature and authority of a true revolutionary or a king, which is why it is difficult for young people to perform.

One student was about to demonstrate the action "to defy," but as he stood on the stage you could see simply from his physical build — he was slight and boyish — that he wasn't ready. His body was static. It was completely lacking in defiance. When he began to speak, his words, though they had fervor, were dead. Every sentence should have had a book behind it, but they were hollow.

His body should have expressed the power and determination behind his defiance, but his body was a lie. It was the body of a little boy, not of a defiant man.

Does that mean he could not — or that you cannot — do the action "to defy?" Of course not. All these actions are in all of us, but we have to find them before we can perform them. To help him find the bodily strength needed for defiance I put another actor on stage with him. I chose a tougher actor to challenge him physically, to butt against him as he delivered his speech. The two actors leaned into each other, but it didn't make the words more powerful. They remained those of a little boy.

I'd been criticizing him, so I thought another way to make the words and body rise in stature might be to confront him myself. I sent the other actor back down, stood in front of the boy and dared him to defy me as I had criticized him. The effect was to make him sarcastic, and I ordered him to stop. Sarcasm is a symptom of weakness, not strength. It's shrinking from confrontation and the very opposite of defiance.

We agreed his nature was passive and he had to work to make his choices more active, more aggressive before he could play roles that required him to perform this action.

Learning to act is a matter of building body and mind to the level where you can perform these actions. Your culture encourages you to remain children long after you should, but you can't be an actor or an actress unless you are an adult.

It's difficult for you to find the largeness required for defiance. Part of the problem is you tend to see actions as merely personal. You don't put them in larger perspectives. When Eliza Doolittle finally defies Henry Higgins, Shaw is not just describing a former flower girl telling off a professor of phonetics. He's writing about the servant class raising itself to the level of its masters. The woman who at the beginning of the play couldn't have imagined herself as anything but a servant is now telling the wealthy, well-born man who has taught her and supported her that she's his equal.

Especially in Shaw, one must hear every word. In her voice the actress must rise with the author. The voice must not drop. At the same time her feet must be planted in the earth. One cannot float above the earth during an act of defiance.

Actors have a tendency to become too emotional when they speak defiantly. This implies a loss of control, which is alien to defiance. Furthermore, especially in Shaw, the words must not get lost in the temperament. To Shaw the words are the most important thing.

I once had a student who, in a class improvisation, attempted to play a black father defying white segregationists determined to prevent his daughter from using a "white only" drinking fountain. He asked five of his fellow students to form a line in front of him. When they were in position he faced them, shaking his fist, and began his speech, "My daughter is going to that fountain, and I'm going down there with her . . ."

I had to stop him. He lost me immediately because he started with the words. He should have started with something his partners gave him, facing him like a wall.

"Start with them," I told him. "Say, 'I don't care if you beat me," or point at each of them and say, '*You're* going to beat me?' and '*You're* going to beat me?' That way you immediately establish your relationship with your partners and set up the words of defiance.

Work on ten actions foreign to your personality. Do this to escape from your personality restrictions, presumably one reason you wanted to be an actor in the first place.

▼

Another action that appears frequently in plays is "to dream." Because it requires losing the present, the action "to dream" is close to the action of reminiscing, but is different because it looks to the future instead of the past. "To dream" is to imagine something you don't have yet but would like to have. It is to see something before you.

It also can be simple. It's Easter, and there's going to be a break from school. You'd love to go to the beach, to have the sun on your body, to plunge into the ocean. You dream of the beach and the sea.

In dreaming you leave your body, much as you do when you sleep. "I'd love to go up into the open sky, with the wind blowing, and look down on the ocean." Your imagination takes control and you lose the present. In the action of dreaming you're not really concerned with where you are. If you're daydreaming in the subway, when the train enters the station you are jolted out of the daydream into reality.

The dream is strong in images and grows in size, expanding with the imagination. To dream requires great energy. Nothing weakens the action more than for the actor's voice to drop. In dreams we soar above our reality, and as soon as there's a falling off in energy the action rings hollow.

A student once was playing the part of a prisoner uttering a dream of freedom. He described the set to us. It consisted of a table, at which he asked another student to sit and play his cell-mate. On the table he placed a portable radio with a collapsible antenna. He then sat down at the table before beginning his monologue. I stopped him immediately.

"That's forbidden," I said. "Never start a scene by sitting down."

I wanted him to use the space before sitting down, to get to know his cell by walking around in it. I asked him to show us one or two things in the cell. Where was the bed? How was it made? I told him to make it an iron cot to see what that would draw out of him.

Once again the things chosen, imaginatively, to fill out and furnish the room were a measure of the student's talent. If in his imagination he could find things to stimulate him, he could do the action. If not, his effort would be merely amateurish.

The student walked around the stage and began to describe his cell in greater detail. "The bed is here," he said. "It's a plain cot with a mattress with stains on it. And here on the wall is a picture of a house with white trim. There is a calendar with days crossed off because the prisoner is about to be released. There is one window, with bars."

I urged him to think about that window. "That window has a life of its own," I said. "A leaf flutters down outside the window. Birds fly past. The last light of day reaches you through it. You worship that window."

Once he'd built the circumstances, he started on his monologue: "Only five more days to go. Then I'll be free. I'll get to sleep on a soft mattress again and I'll wear silk pajamas and I'll be able to sleep as long as I want in the morning and stay up as late as I want at night."

He picked up the portable radio and showed it to his cell-mate. "I'm going to start a radio repair shop and fix radios and TV sets for little old ladies."

This was correct. Dreaming with another person next to you is not possible unless at some point you leave the dream and address the person directly. If a partner is present, you have to divide the dream.

The choice of the radio as a prop was unfortunate. A mechanical object leads to mechanical acting. The dream itself, which was about soft mattresses and silk pajamas and sleeping late, was too comfortably middle class. It lacked drama.

As long as he'd chosen the radio I urged him to make the dream about a repair shop, about mending broken things. Then it would have mattered.

▼

An important action is "to pray." It comes at the end of a succession of other actions, to ask, to beg, to plead. Each is stronger than the last, and each depends on the relationship between the person making the request and the person he is petitioning. When I ask something of you, it implies we're on the same level. When I beg or plead it implies you have more power and consequently I must abase myself.

"To pray" is the final progression in this series. There are different kinds of prayer. In *Misalliance* Shaw has one of his characters ask a Polish aviatrix what she asks for when she prays. She reprimands him that she doesn't ask for things. "I pray to remind myself I have a soul," she tells him.

Nevertheless many prayers are a reaching out for help, for consolation. You're begging for help, and in this case you are pleading with someone whose power is infinite.

A good exercise for this action is to suppose you're an Egyptian peasant praying to the gods for rain. This action is foreign to you for a number of reasons. You're most likely not used to praying, and especially not for rain. You cajole your super to fix your faucets. So you have to build circumstances that agitate you. You could say, "Please, God, send rain because the children are without water."

Next imagine the children. See them with their eyes red and their tongues swollen. The circumstances are now alive, and the action becomes real. The need to pray is urgent.

If you can reach out to one god, you can seek help from any god.

As an exercise create four imaginative situations in which you have to reach out to something higher for help. Pray to Zeus, pray to Buddha. Be aware of praying differently to different images. Pray to get help, to give thanks, to beg for relief.

Take three different actions (to pray, to grieve, to argue) and do them in three different centuries: the Greek period, the 18th century, the 19th century.

And don't pray to me! I expect you to do it all on your own.

UNDERSTANDING THE TEXT

S o far we have worked on exercises to enliven our imagination, to give us size, to equip us with a vocabulary of actions. We've been trying to develop our ability to see and understand. We've worked on actions and seen how important it is to justify our every action. But an audience doesn't come to the theatre to see our exercises. They come to see plays.

They want to see the actor display himself, but not the way a model displays himself or herself, as a backdrop for clothes. We may see the actor in costume, and in a world totally unlike ours, more glamorous, more magical or more sordid. But the communication the actor makes isn't about these mere artifacts.

We say the actor is on display, but what we mean is he's displaying what's inside him. More precisely, he's displaying the insides of his character. All our previous efforts have been moving toward helping us play characters.

Acting is human behavior assembled in novel and interesting ways. Even an archetypal figure like Hamlet can be portrayed in hundreds of new and exciting character interpretations — as a revolutionary, a coward, a romantic, an intellectual, even an Oedipal mess: such was John Barrymore's notion.

An essential element of acting is delineating the differences between people, or character. An Italian designer, a Russian peasant and a Chinese diplomat all behave in different ways.

They hold themselves differently, walk, talk, think, smoke cigarettes and laugh differently. Their backgrounds, education, physical manner, moralities and conditioning are wholly dissimilar. The actor, however, is not only to reproduce these national and occupational traits. He must also show the differences between individuals — how two Italian designers, for instance, behave differently toward the same attractive client.

▼

We may start with the outside, the external part, but we have to move inward.

This is necessitated by the plays written over the last hundred years. If you perform Shakespeare everything you need to know is in the lines. You're a better actor if you go beneath the lines, but in Shakespeare everything is in the words.

In the first scene of *Romeo and Juliet* there's a fight in the street. Juliet's father says, "What noise is this? Give me my long sword, ho!" His wife says, "A crutch, a crutch! Why call you for a sword?" What more do you need to know about the Capulets?

That is not true of playwrights after Ibsen. Mr. Stanislavski was forced to develop the techniques he did because he acted in plays in which you couldn't do otherwise. You cannot play Chekhov from the lines alone. There is no way in which you can play Ibsen in his lines, or Strindberg or Tennessee Williams . . . or Odets.

You cannot. It simply isn't there to be done. They do not write that way. They do not create character that way.

The acting rather is in you, not in the printed words. The actor's interpretations of these words must be clear and sharp. He starts with words but then must go beneath them. Texts must be examined. They have a secret under and around the words. An actor is one who uncovers and incorporates the secrets of words.

▼

One of our first exercises was to take a text by Kahlil Gibran and paraphrase it. This is something we must do with every text. Paraphrasing allows the ideas to become part of you. By putting the text into your own words you build a relationship with it. It becomes part of your heart as well as your head, which is essential before you can communicate the words to an audience. If the ideas are clear to you they will be clear to them.

When you've understood the text's ideas, when you've mastered them, made them your own, *then* you can go back to the words. You can now look at them fresh. You can see beyond the periods and the commas and the exclamation points, which only get in the way. If you're bound by punctuation marks, work in a library, not the theatre.

The playwright gives you more than words. He gives you circumstances. Every play is written out of a social situation. If you don't understand the social situation you'll be playing from a blind spot. We no longer have a theatre where you can just play types. A century ago you joined a troupe and played a type. You fit the type. You were chosen because you *were* the type.

That's not acting. Acting is only when you *refuse* to use yourself as the character. In the entire history of acting, nobody played himself. There is no such thing in the history of acting as Henry Irving playing Mr. Irving. Outside the theatre is perhaps another matter. But inside, never! They all played characters.

Characters come out of social situations. The social situation is what leads you into depth. Every man lives in his own time. Every man comes from a specific economic situation. Every man lives in a religious atmosphere, if it exists, if he wants it, even if he doesn't want it.

Every man lives in the moral situation of his moment. What is his moral situation? Does he believe the family should be kept together? Does he believe in divorce? Does he believe in abortion?

Every man is subject to a political situation. What is your character? How did it grow? The social situation is what has created the human being throughout history. Hermits do not need to put on plays for themselves.

If you're playing "a father," you're still not playing a type. You have to ask, "Where did this father come from?" Is he Hamlet's father? Hamlet's father had a kingdom. He created a dynasty. He needed a son to carry it on. Is he Strindberg's character in *The Father*? Strindberg's Father is enormously challenged by his position in life. His authority is threatened.

Strindberg's Father finds his authority threatened in a strongly militaristic society, where the position of men is very strong, where the authority of masculinity is at its height. Yet he is threatened.

Is your father one who lives after World War II in a small house in Brooklyn, where he's trying to raise two sons but his income as a salesman is failing him? Willy Loman is as much a father as he is a salesman.

All these fathers are entirely different from one another. Each has to be understood in his own social setting. Hamlet's father needs to be a certain kind of father for his time. Strindberg's Father has certain problems. The father in Arthur Miller's *Death of a Salesman* has other problems.

Unless I know the social situation, I don't know how to think about the character. I just don't know what to do with him. You know, I'm not very smart except in this. God looked down and said, "Stella, you're smart." Outside of that, I'm stupid.

▼

So the first thing that saves you from being stranded with the play's words is understanding the social situation. From the words you can grab hold of the plot. From the plot you'll get one or two things that interest you, stimulate you, light you up.

But don't let the words dominate you because they can only give you the *convention* of a human being. You avoid the convention, the type, by going to the society that created this man, going to the character's past, the plot's past.

A human being, if you take him out of his social situation is somebody else. He doesn't know who he is, and neither will you know how to play him because you're in limbo.

So know what political era it is, what country it is, what time it is. Your curse is that you chose a form that requires endless study. And that, take it or leave it, is *your* social situation, should anyone ever write a play about you.

It's also your obligation to give the playwright's ideas universality and epic size. You have to convey the bigness of what the playwright's saying. Suppose you're describing an everyday occurrence, such as a boy chasing a ball blown by the wind. You enlarge the meaning by adding the idea that the child wants to keep up with the wind, that the child can play games with nature, that nature is stronger than man.

The pull of the play is always toward some large theme and the danger we fall into is making it small. The modern play questions life, questions what to do about it, questions how we must live. So the actor must get used to giving ideas size by learning to deal with universal questions, the questions that have been around for a long time — questions of love, loyalty and friendship, of family and children. To be articulate about such ideas and to be effective in communicating them is your responsibility.

▼

Here's a good exercise about controlling the size of a play. Imagine a man visiting a prisoner, giving the prisoner the following line: "If it were not for you, I wouldn't be here." The circumstances, then, are the prison. The plot is that the man who has betrayed the prisoner has come to see him. The exercise is to continue the dialogue and create the play. One student playing the visitor supplied the following line: "Oh, you'll be out of here by Christmas."

I told him he had lowered the play to its smallest meaning. Do you see? The drama had been leached out. We should be looking for the epic quality of any situation.

All through the ages man has been guilty, and betrayal is the worst of his sins. He must face his guilt. He visits the prisoner to seek release from his torture. In other words, the exercise of the actor is to make the play bigger — and avoid making it inconsequential and trivial.

In another class exercise about a bully, an actor adopted a pugnacious tone. "You had to fink on me," he told his partner. "I never knew you were on their side. You disgust me."

Because he lacked size, the student had seized on exactly the tone to be kept out. The actor may find it easy to insult another person when he doesn't care enough to insult a system or God. He had a "tough kid" kind of anger in him.

I advised him — and I advise you — to watch a great actor like Luther Adler or Marlon Brando show anger on stage. The explosion is monumental, because seven-eighths of it is underneath. In the student eight-eighths was on the surface. No real anger lay underneath. His anger was like a taxi driver's — loud, verbose and ineffective. Better by far to be angry with God or with mankind than have this cheap "chip-on-the-shoulder" "you-lost-I-won" sort of anger.

Better by far to reverse it and say, "You lost your way and I lost mine," rather than "If I fight you, I win and you lose." The English have a superior sense of what a game is. When the English play cricket, they want to win, but if they do, they don't feel the other fellow has lost. They've played a game. There's no real winning or losing. This is precisely what's wrong with the American spirit of competition. We feel that if we win, the opponent is a failure.

Raise the contest and the anger to an epic level. When Stanley Kowalski gets angry in *A Streetcar Named Desire*, he wants to destroy the spirit of man because it's something he can't attain. He sets out to destroy Blanche Dubois because he lacks her spiritual strength. Out of anger and enraged frustration he attacks what he cannot have.

Look for the author's central idea — the big Why? — and find the universal content of the play. One of our first exercises was to look for things we consider ordinary but which are universal and eternal. Small facts of life will reveal the large meaning. Immense size comes from understanding your relationship to everything you come into contact with — ideas, people, objects, experiences.

When a playwright writes about two classes of people, as Shaw does in *Pygmalion*, the play has significance. The theme is Eliza's fight for freedom against someone who has pushed her down. She's saying to a whole class, "You have had too much, and we have had too little."

As an actor, your presentation of the idea must be as large as the idea itself. Don't be afraid to use your voice and your body. Give me your energy, give me an idea you'd fight for. Enrich the audience. Don't leave them empty-handed or with small ideas.

▼

Your task when you approach a text, whether it is Shakespeare, Tennessee Williams or a television show, is to take it inside you before giving it back from the stage. You must first identify the text's idea and understand how it develops. The idea leads you to sequences, to a series of interconnected points.

Look for the sequence and follow it to see how the idea develops. Let one sequence lead you to another. A monologue can build from a high emotional moment to a low one; or from down to up, or from the middle. By tracing the sequence one discovers the progression.

Here's Eliza Doolittle in Act V of Shaw's *Pygmalion*, when she comes to the angry realization that all the time she's been used by Henry Higgins:

"What a fool I was not to think of it before. You can't take away the knowledge you gave me — you said I had a finer ear than you. And I can be civil and kind to people, which is more than you can. Aha, that's done you, Henry Higgins — it has. Now I don't care *that* — for your bullying and your big talk. I'll advertise it in the papers that your Duchess is only a flower girl that you taught and she'll teach anybody to be a duchess just the same in six months for a thousand guineas. Oh! When I think of myself crawling under your feet and being trampled and called names when all the time I had only to lift up my finger to be as good as you, I could kick myself."

Eliza's monologue builds from the high emotional moment of her realization that she's just as good as Henry Higgins to the low one of wanting to kick herself for permitting him to trample her. The sequences we can trace are:

(1) Now I know I'm just as good as you.

(2) I could expose your trickery in creating a duchess out of a flower girl if I wanted to.

(3) I could kick myself for permitting you to bully me.

The strongest base for a table is three legs. If you can find three interrelated ideas in a text you have a play that's in control.

In one classroom exercise a student made a speech about improving conditions in a city. She made three points. Her first was that businesses suffered because the streets were badly lit. Second, a group of businessmen got together to contribute money toward better lighting. Third, their efforts were so successful the mayor decided to increase the city budget for street lamps.

Seeing the images will help you understand what you're talking about. If you see the stores along the dimly lit streets where the people are afraid to walk you'll understand why the businessmen wanted to do something. If you see the same streets now well lit and the people gayer you'll understand why business picked up.

Seeing helps the student care about her theme. The city is going to improve. It will be a more prosperous and better place. The success of the student's presentation comes from dividing the theme into three points, each following from the other.

Go from sequence to sequence in a text, not from sentence to sentence. Don't put in periods or commas. By the sense of the text and by your identification of the sequences, you introduce your own periods and commas.

Most of us were taught to read when we were too little to understand what we read. The period was there to make sense for us. You'll find your own place for the period, depending on where the sequences fall. The period stops the sequence, but as long as you know where the sequence starts and finishes, it doesn't matter where the periods fall.

▼

We've spent a lot of time working on actions and on using the imagination to make actions our own. We've spent time on using the imagination to make props and costumes ours. If I ask you to sip coffee out of a paper cup and then out of a porcelain demitasse cup, I'm asking you to understand two very different worlds. That's the kind of effort we have to make every time we approach a character.

To create a character on stage you must have a fully realized past for that character. You must imagine in detail the early life, family history, educational training, professional experience and personal relationships. This is the first thing you prepare when you work on a character.

Background is created out of the five W's — who, what, where, when, why. Answer these questions and the background falls into place. For instance, imagine a bunch of daffodils you've received from a friend.

They live in a vase in your living room for five days, and then you throw them out with the trash. When you received the daffodils, they'd already lived a life of their own. They were born in a nursery in Holland and were transplanted to grow in special soil. They were sent to the flower market in Amsterdam and bought at the flower auction. They were loaded onto a plane as air freight and shipped to Kennedy Airport. From there they went first to a wholesale florist on 28th Street and then to the flower shop in the Village where your friend spotted them. You now know the what, where, when and why of the daffodil. If called upon, you could now play one of the daffodils.

You have to understand the same background details about every character you play. The background should suggest why you're doing what you're doing.

Several factors in particular play a crucial role in shaping character. One is profession. The other is class. Let's start with profession. Americans admit to professions. They don't admit to classes. One of the problems with American acting today, in fact, is that it's classless. American actors think they can ignore class even if they know they can't ignore profession.

Always work from a profession. The profession most of you find yourself in is student. It governs a great deal of what you do, and, of course, what you don't do.

You must see that even begging is a profession. The panhandler in the street doesn't behave randomly. How does he do it? What is his technique? Does he approach everybody? Does he know who people are? Does he judge? Does he think? Is he proud of his profession?

You have to *do* something. If you *do* something, you become somebody. Even a daffodil does something, has a profession. It gives off scent, professionally.

When you come in saying, "I'm a lawyer" or "I'm a doctor" or "I'm a stenographer," you're somebody that *does* something. You don't come in with lines. You don't come in with a scene. You come in as somebody who does something. What do *you* do? Think about it.

In studying a character, almost the first question to ask is: what's his or her profession? It's the "who" in the sequence of preconditions — who, what, when, where, why — that must be settled before an action can be performed. You have a profession. What do you profess? You should be able to tell me the ideas you profess, the values you profess, all based on your profession. Do you see?

The study of professions has a number of side benefits. When you are forced to go into the everyday world to study the profession of the person you're playing you train yourself to be observant.

The authority you develop in observing and playing a profession rubs off on your personal life and increases your confidence. The vague, floating quality one associates with a student actor disappears. It is replaced by a new assurance. Professions also lead the young actor naturally into the character, for what you do is what you are.

▼

The technique for playing a profession is simple: Build up a believable past in that profession, and, through imagined biographical data, to know how you came to be in it and who you are in it. Your inner attitude will advance your action. The core of being a professional is to be sure of what you're doing, to know it so well that you're always in control. A no-nonsense approach to the work is a sure sign of a professional. Isn't it? If you have a sense of who you are, your activities will reflect this self-assurance.

As a learning exercise it's better for you to choose a profession you must go out and observe rather than something close to you. Study the professionalism of certain crafts such as printer, typesetter, hairdresser, machinist, sailor, nurse, carpenter, prostitute, miller, nun. As far as possible the profession should contain costume and props befitting the job.

But not too many props. One day a student came in laden with camera equipment — two cameras strapped across his shoulders, a camera bag, a tripod. Portraying a combat photographer, he dashed across the stage in the midst of presumed gunfire, flopped onto his belly and aimed his camera at the audience.

The tripod fell, clattering to the stage, and he paused to pick it up. Resuming his picture-taking, he stopped himself, dove in another direction and re-aimed. It was a noisy, cluttered, undisciplined performance. One had no feeling that he was in command of his profession. The audience felt he was a professional clown.

The camera is a scientific instrument. It is made to catch the moment. He faked the moment. He faked the action. He was hysterical instead of controlled. He fell, but he didn't know *how* to fall.

The dropped tripod was an unplanned accident. That's something that should never happen on stage. You cannot have an accident on the stage without carefully planning it beforehand. The accident may come as a surprise to the audience, but it cannot come as a surprise to the actor. The actor must always be in control of his props.

"I didn't believe it was a battle," I told him. "You just threw yourself down. I want to see a man working as a photographer. Craftsmanship is what I want, not drama. Drama develops out of the craft. You were photographing a battle. You were in danger. I saw that. But you clicked your camera without seeing anything.

"Your whole body was tense, and you were making believe there was a war. In the school of realistic drama, you want to convey a way of life. You don't want to convey a plot."

I suggested this student switch subjects to something less dramatic than combat photography, to photographing the architecture of the room. When he did, the whole rhythm of the action changed.

When you have a profession in a play, you let the profession give you a rhythm that's not your own. Often the doing of the profession takes time in rehearsal because it's not developed until it's been done over and over.

Who has a profession to show us? All right, Bobby. What is it?

BOBBY: I'm going to play a professor.

STELLA: A professor of what?

BOBBY: A professor of English.

STELLA: I'm frightened of the physical limitations when you take that kind of profession. But go ahead.

BOBBY: Good morning, class. Today we're going to study . . .

STELLA: I have to stop you. You're moving around the stage in a supposedly professorial manner, but the rhythm is boring. Also, you haven't demonstrated any reason for where you're going. Your walk is a shuffle, the bottoms of your feet never leave the ground. We can correct the walk but I doubt we can salvage the profession. Take a profession where you *do* something, not a profession where we have to guess what you're doing.

Who else has a profession? All right, Sal, go up on stage. What's good about Sal is his costume. He has an electrician's belt slung from his waist that has the tools of his trade — screwdriver, wirecutters, measuring tape, needle-nose pliers.

Now what's he doing? It looks like he's untangling a web of wires. You're taking too long in the same space, Sal. Remember the work we did on smartening up actions. If you want us to see that something doesn't work, you must make it not work. You took props that controlled you completely.

Your appearance is also wrong for the profession you chose. For a worker's face and hands, yours are too clean. You should have dust on your arms, dirt on your hands and, possibly, a rag appearing from the pocket of your pants.

Who wants to be next? All right, Sally. What's your profession?

SALLY: Librarian.

STELLA: Well, we can see that you're a librarian by the bundle of books you're carrying. My concern is your costume. Costume can be used subtly or clumsily to reveal a profession. You have a colored blouse and white stockings. To begin with, there are too many props, but it's the clothes that struck the jarring note. They're the wrong shade. I don't see a librarian when I see you. You should be all one color. The books are the colors. You should be as a blotter behind them. In this exercise the more you're playing to the audience, trying to impress them, the less successful you are.

All right, who wants to be next? John.

What is John doing? He has put out a row of glasses on a cabinet he had set up on the stage. Behind them he has placed two brass candlesticks and a brass flower vase. He's rested a clipboard on a table where he can retrieve it easily. In a foil of paper on a side table is a white gardenia.

JOHN: My profession is that of the second-floor department manager at Tiffany's.

STELLA: So far, so good, John.

What's he doing now? He's counting articles, arranging them, inspecting the glasses, inspecting the candlesticks, checking them off on his clipboard, putting out a lettered sign that says the items displayed were on sale. Very good, John.

Now he's crossing the stage to the side table and taking the gardenia out of its roll of paper. He fits the flower into the button hole of his jacket and walks back to the display counter. Inspecting the glasses once again, he takes his handkerchief out of his breast pocket and begins polishing the glasses.

Wrong! That's your first major mistake. A department manager wouldn't wipe the glasses with his own handkerchief. He would have used a cloth.

Furthermore, I have the impression that overall you're performing too obviously for us, the audience. You're stage forward all the time. You're saying, "Look at me, look at me." Anything in your manner that's stagey, anything the slightest bit theatrical or done to *show* the audience turns into falsehood.

Here's an adjustment — turn your back to the audience. It's a simple enough change, but it will force you to concentrate on the objects and on what you're doing. It will make your actions more truthful.

It's a paradox of the theatre that the more you do it for the audience, the less they want it. It's what made Willy Loman a lousy salesman. He was too eager.

▼

A lot of what you do to prepare isn't seen at all. When we look at those daffodils we see the color, the shape, we don't know they were grown in Holland. With the flowers it doesn't matter. Only what you see matters. That is not true with characters. You must know the background detail.

Before you can live convincingly in the present on the stage, you must have a fully realized past. It's the first thing an actor should do when preparing a character.

Let's take a shop manager. First we must determine what kind of shop he manages. Let's make it an antique shop. This dictates immediately a kind of dress. The manager is dressed formally because the shop was built on old-world traditions.

There are certain things it is logical to say about him:

He was very efficient, since he was brought up in Europe, where education is more rigorous.

He knew the value of every item in the store.

He was a serious man, which means, in acting terms, he could lecture on the antiques in his store. One cannot play "serious." The actor must find an action that will convey the seriousness.

He'd go home and discuss various articles with his father, who was also an antique dealer. And just as serious.

These are things we know about him now, but we can also build him a believable and useful past:

His family lived among old-world artifacts.

His father realized when, as a child, the boy became interested in antiques he should be instructed in languages.

When he came home from school he'd always look forward to playing games with his father with the words he'd learned. His father would have him put all his new words into sentences.

He was not without mischievousness. He would tease his father, telling him he wanted to be a cowboy when he grew up.

Every day, he'd read aloud with his father before dinner. Dinner was *very* formal. He had to dress for it. He and his mother would converse at dinnertime. His mother was very interested in what he'd accomplished. He'd proudly tell her what he'd learned that day.

She'd be so proud of him she'd give him presents — extra chocolates or a new set of pencils. She was delighted when, as he grew up, he'd explain to her the different styles of crystal and would teach her the difference in the patterns of silver. She started to become a scholar, like her son and husband.

Both the boy and his father enjoyed watching this development. He was proud of his mother. She would talk to a customer about the value of crystal, and when she'd make a big sale — because crystal was very antique and very special — they'd all go to a nice restaurant for dinner.

When he was eighteen, he got his first taste of wine. They decided then there ought always to be wine at the dinner table at home.

He became meticulous about what he knew. He'd read, spend most of his free time doing research, both at school and at home. He understood that to get work he needed to look like a European sales manager.

His clothes became English in style. He fussed over how his shirts were pressed and how his shoes were polished.

He was cheerful and good-natured. When customers had no idea what they wanted to buy, he'd help them decide.

When we see him he's 21 and other shop managers depend on his knowledge of crystal and silver.

A good exercise to prepare to play our shop manager is to draw the circumstances of his shop on a piece of paper, to lay out the acting space. Then put the space in your mind and use it when rehearsing in your own room.

Walk around in the circumstances of the shop: (a) shelves with objects you can describe in detail; (b) a table with a group of intriguing antiques; (c) a desk on which you write orders, and (d) two chairs of different styles.

Be able to discuss the way the shop manager behaves away from his job — at home, among intimate friends, socially.

▼

What we did with the shop manager we must do with other professions. How would you use the stage if you were a gardener, a painter, a college student?

Observe the action that people display from morning to night. Watch them in a church, in a hotel lobby, in a bank, in a department store. Study the professionalism of certain crafts and how it affects the character's non-professional life. Observe those actions away from the circumstances of the job — at home, among friends, playing a sport.

Determine in what manner a professional performs his functions. Is he nervous, good-natured, sloppy, organized, carefree, meticulous?

Ignore no aspect of your character's life, unless you want the gaps to crop up some night on stage.

CHARACTER ELEMENTS

First and foremost, when you get a job, read the text of the play to determine what ideas the playwright wants to give to the world.

Nowadays we have a rather trivial idea of the theatre. We also have the stinkingest audience in the world — they don't know who the actors are, they certainly don't know who the playwrights are. But when the great playwrights sat down to write their plays their intention wasn't just to amuse an ignorant audience. The theatre was a platform to address the world, and the actor the means.

The actor must discover what ideas the playwright wants to reveal through his characters. Although a play may be set in a particular locale, it's meant to reach the world. The reason I constantly stress that you must have size on stage is because that's what the playwright requires to convey his ideas. The more vivid you can make his characters, the more interesting and far-reaching his ideas will be.

One way we can build a character is by identifying character elements the playwright uses in creating his people. Here's a list of character elements that are worth studying:

- Carefree
- Outgoing
- Ambitious
- Enterprising

- Responsible
- Adventurous
- Reliable
- Introspective
- Conscientious
- Scholarly
- Practical

You can draw upon the world for deep knowledge of the character elements. You watch these elements and then you put them into circumstances that are true for you.

By taking elements you observe in life, you can develop qualities in your acting life that you don't ordinarily call upon in your personal life.

▼

Let's start with "carefree." A very good way to observe this element is to study birds. A bird can land anywhere — on the limb of a high tree, on a chimney, a lamppost, a bush, or a rock.

If you had to play a carefree boy, you could imagine him hopping on a bike, sliding down a bannister, swinging around a lamppost or leaping over a fire hydrant. He might jump into a pool fully clothed or fully unclothed. He might come to a formal party in a jogging outfit. When he encounters friends he flings his arms around them.

He's animated, lively, in continuous movement. The element "carefree" also has in it a lack of logic, a lack of responsibility to the outside world, a sense of being unfixed in life. His actions have the rhythm of positive aimlessness.

The opposite of carefree is "reliable." What animal can you study to see reliability? A well-trained dog is entirely reliable, entirely dependable. As an exercise, imagine yourself in a situation calling for reliability. Don't be general. Find a physical action that demonstrates this trait.

Another character element worth exploring is "meticulous." A profession that requires a meticulous character is medicine.

When a doctor examines a patient he must be meticulous. When he washes his hands both before and after surgery, he's being meticulous.

I myself am extremely careless about everything in my personal life. I once put some eggs in a frying pan, turned on the stove and left the house. It's true. That is why many people think I should never be allowed anywhere near a kitchen. Nevertheless I can say I'm meticulous in my stage life. Nothing is where it shouldn't be.

In playing a part, I draw upon the deep knowledge of this meticulousness. By exploring certain personal elements, you can even develop qualities you don't regularly depend upon.

▼

Actors are undercover agents. You must constantly spy on people, studying their character elements. You must see which are related to the character's profession or appropriate to his nationality or age. Acting is hard because it requires not just the study of books, though that can be important too, but constant study of human behavior.

One dependable comfort is that you are never alone on stage. You have the circumstances of the play to work with. You have the set. You have your props and your costume.

You also have your fellow actors.

You always have partners on stage, and you have an attitude toward your partner. In all cases your partner is needed to give you your action; and you have to know the partner's attitude toward everything. Dialogue exists not on cue but when you understand and react to your partner.

I'm going to select two actors from the class and ask them to go up on stage and play two monkeys living in the same cage. Certain behavioral traits will very soon appear. Each monkey will shortly develop an attitude toward the other, whether it's hostility, jealousy, affection or some other response.

Resist the tendency to start acting right away. Let the action come from some place that prompts it. Beware of behavioral cliches ("monkey business"), don't start fighting before fighting is actually justified — that is, before either has taken any action against the other. If one snatches a banana away from the other, then the anger is provoked, and the fighting will be more interesting.

Acting is reacting, and shouldn't arise out of a false response. And the reacting always presumes the presence of a partner.

Actually, the two monkeys, before they do anything together, should live for a time separately, so that each develops an individual character. Allow an opinion of the other to form slowly and naturally. The attitude will develop, and the audience will develop its attitude toward the characters.

Now let's put a few more actors on the stage and divide them up between dogs and chickens. Find some way to relate to each other. First, each group of animals must learn to live in its circumstances. Is it a farmyard? If so, the attitude will be different than an open field.

In any case, the attitude between you should not be combative. Since fighting is the cheapest thing you can do on stage, it's better to use your imagination and find some other obvious way dogs and chickens can live together. If the dogs refrain from bothering the chickens, it will be more interesting, and real attitudes will emerge.

What you think of a person stimulates you to behave in a certain way toward him. Herein lies the wisdom of acting. It's not what a person says but your reaction to what he says that creates your attitude toward the person. Without this attitude you don't exist on the stage.

What does it mean to have an attitude toward your partner and where does it come from? From your reactions to what you see, what confronts you, what you're exposed to.

We can illustrate this on the most primitive level. If you see a snake on the ground, would you go over and pick it up? Having already developed an attitude toward the snake, from what you know or have heard or read about snakes, going back to the earliest Biblical reference, you wouldn't.

One develops an attitude toward everything — even toward the snake. As an intern at the hospital, you quickly become aware the operation has failed. Your actions are to check the X-rays, the patient's chart and the EKG. You see everything's gone wrong. Now you have an attitude toward the doctor in charge.

Suppose you have a very wealthy friend. Her husband, whom she didn't much care for, has died. In his memory she gives money to various institutions and dedicates a number of memorials to him. Now she wants to remarry, but not for love. She wants a companion.

How do you feel about her? One attitude might be you'd like to exploit her money yourself. We can add a little information. She likes to give parties and even invites people she doesn't know well. She is regularly accustomed to spending $400 or $500 a night inviting people to dinner. What do you really think of her? Are you developing an attitude toward her? Do you think her values are distorted, or that she's lonely, or do you resent her money? Do you feel she's mixed up, wasteful and stupid?

Now suppose, to bring it closer to home, this woman comes to me and says she wants to direct a play using the students in this class for the cast. My reaction to her proposal is: Why not? She has money. Why shouldn't she direct a play? I invite her to come and direct members of this class in a play. What would your reaction be?

She wants to be treated professionally. She asks the actors to take minimum pay since none is a member of Actors Equity. After the performance, she also wants to give a lecture on the playwright. I agree to all her conditions.

Now which of you wants to be in this woman's play. Not so

fast. And not so emotional. What's that? To allow a woman to buy her way in is opposed to everything the theatre stands for — it's selling out. I see. Brad, what do you think? That you feel perfectly capable of taking from the woman's direction what's right and helpful and leaving out what's useless. So you think it's all right for her to come.

Isn't it interesting that each of you has developed an attitude toward this woman before she has even appeared and thus a drama has been created.

By the variety of our responses to the way people express themselves, we develop an attitude toward a person. If I say, "Oh, no, I wish I could come, but I can't," that expresses one attitude. The attitude changes when you say, "Oh, I do wish I could come, darling. I can't." The first is sincere and felt. The second is less genuine, even a little false.

In a play you can't really work unless you develop an attitude toward your partner.

To speak on stage you must be provoked by something that will *make* you speak. Unless somebody says something or you hear a noise or you're stimulated in some other way, you must not speak. In saying a line, your natural tendency is to wait for an answer. This is called "sitting on your partner." It's something you mustn't do. Don't wait for the dialogue, and don't suddenly push your partner into an answer. As you exchange dialogue, thoughts of your own can come, unexpectedly. For example, in the country, I said to my husband one day, "It's too cold. I don't want the dog to go out. Did they ever catch the man who killed Lincoln?"

This last has nothing to do with what we were talking about, but it's natural to have irrelevant thoughts, even though they may come as a complete surprise to your partner. If you actually talk to him, he must answer. But if you simply say something not conditioned on a response, he may or may not answer you.

Each time you must react as if for the first time. Each time, you must create the images that lead you to speak while adhering to the theme and reacting to your partner. If you remain with the theme and never fail to respond to the partner, you have a play.

Resist the impulse to make the play fit you. You must fit the play.

As an example of how to build an attitude toward a partner almost unconsciously, I propose the following: a director is putting on a play with three students, you, you and you. There is a woman assistant director, and a stage manager, who's a man. Now only respond yes or no to the following questions. Shout out your answers. I don't expect you to agree.

(1) Does the stage manager confer with the director?

(2) Does the director need the stage manager?

(3) Do they eat together?

(4) Does the assistant director talk to the director much?

(5) Does the director let the assistant director take rehearsal?

(6) Does she want to take rehearsal?

And so on. Even with only a positive or negative response, you can see how quickly your attitudes are built, perhaps in some cases based on past experience with these characters' real-life counterparts.

Carrying the theatrical metaphor a step further, let's put together a summer repertory company. I want six students to come up on the stage. Now I want each of you to tell the rest of us how you would spend the summer. Based on their responses, we will vote on who gets each job in the summer repertory company.

The jobs are:

(1) box office treasurer, to handle the money, pay the bills and balance the books;

(2) public relations manager, a job of handling VIPs and arranging press parties;

(3) stage manager, responsible for making up all the time schedules;

(4) artistic director and literary advisor, who chooses the plays and directs them;

(5) an understudy for all the men's parts;

(6) an understudy for all the women's parts.

Okay, the votes are in. Why did you vote for a particular person for a particular job? Sum up the character element, put the character element into an action, and put the character traits into various circumstances.

It wasn't hard, was it? The actor who said he'd spend his summer writing we made the dramaturg. You said he should concentrate on the character element "scholarly." The character traits you associated with him were absentminded and untrimmed. Sally wanted to organize a jazz radio station as her summer project. So we made her the public relations manager. The character element they suggested she focus on was "outgoing."

Billy said he'd spend the summer relaxing and enjoying himself. They identified his character element as "carefree." Billy, you didn't get any job.

John was going to spend the summer studying investments, so we made him the box office manager. The character element for John was to be conservative. To put the conservative element in action, when the show turns out to be a hit and the director asks you to order tickets for a month in advance, what will you do, John? That's right, you'll only order tickets for two weeks ahead just in case the audience drops off. Very good.

▼

Here's another exercise to help us understand attitude toward the partner. An actress and an architect share an apartment and a bit more than that.

The actress wants to have a party in the apartment for her friends. The architect wants to come home to a quiet place and work. The actress discovers the liquor she ordered for the party has been returned to the store.

A quarrel breaks out between them over money and the moral issues involved in their very different life-styles. The architect asks the actress to leave. He views her as disastrously misguided and self-defeating.

What emerges from their argument are two distinct points of view, the realist and the artist. She assails his principles, his need for success, his unimaginative middle-class life. But she is partially dependent on him to cover her expenses when she's not working. She even expected him to pay for the liquor.

He predicts failure for her given way of life as well as perpetual artistic insecurity. Her action is to accept her way of life and warn him about the limitations of his. She criticizes his fussy tidyness, his lack of liveliness and stimulation, his exaggerated self-control. He criticizes her friends, her way of dressing, her undisciplined way of life.

In her own defense, the actress argues it's not every night that she throws a party, that she studies diligently and goes to dance classes. She's up for a part with an acting company that will be performing out of town. She's misunderstood.

The architect maintains he doesn't need to understand anything about her position. He argues the apartment is his office, his work is important and she assumes too many privileges in the name of art. He recently lent money to one of her actor friends whose wallet was stolen. With a laxity typical of the profession, he never made good.

In summary, the actress says, in effect: I can get along on the outside. I learn from the world. I need people and need to be involved with people. One can't plan ahead. It's hopeless to try. There are no guarantees.

The architect says: I learn from books. My work fulfills me. I don't need people. I'm not afraid to be alone. I plan and I must have order. I know there are no guarantees, but I must go on anyway and do my best.

The action of the actress is to give a party. Within this action are these steps: (a) to arrange the room, (b) to put out the food, and (c) to get herself ready. The action of the architect is to complete his important project.

In staging this little play we might allot one minute to the actress to prepare the party, one minute for the architect to come home to work, two minutes for the actress to discover the missing liquor and to confront the architect with this discovery, and then several minutes for the ensuing discussion of their differing ways of life.

The drama emerges from the attitude of the actress toward the architect and vice-versa.

Schematically, their differences might be expressed as follows:

ACTRESS	*ARCHITECT*
Risks security for inner growth	Wants security
Truth of life within herself	Compromises
Main overall action: To live one's theatrical life	Main overall action: To control one's life
Actions:	*Actions:*
(1) to prepare for party	(1) to prepare for work

(2) to discuss lifestyle   (2) to discuss lifestyle

(3) to predict partner's   (3) to predict partner's
    future   future

In order to play the actress or the architect, and show the deep rift between them, all this background work is essential. Only when it's accomplished will you have paid the price for what you are and what you want and only then will you be able to lift the discussion to its highest level — to the overall importance of art versus commerce.

▼

Exaggerated in justification, past experience can be cooled when you speak in the present, but first you'll have paid the price. The words come only on top of this past experience, and it's the culmination of your work as an actor. The larger your down payment on preparation, the greater your investment in the past, the more you'll believe and the more understanding you'll have. On that sure foundation can be built attitudes and conflicts.

In all cases, your partner is needed to give you your action, and you need to know your partner's attitude toward everything. Again, and not for the last time, dialogue exists not on cue but when you understand and react to your partner.

Working on this exercise, you should be able to play both sides.

DRESSING THE PART

I'll begin by asking six men to stand on the stage about two feet from each other. What can the rest of us say about the way they're dressed? Is it attractive? Not particularly. It's neat. It's clean. Is it *soignee?* Not at all. It's comfortable, casual.

Do they dress as their fathers would have dressed? It depends on their fathers' ages. If their fathers grew up in the Fifties, very likely they'd still have worn jackets and ties. They didn't wear earrings. They didn't wear boots. They didn't wear sneakers. If their fathers grew up in the Sixties they might dress very much like these young men.

Actors must develop the ability to see even casual dress as something historical. To wear a shirt the way they do, with the sleeves rolled up or more than one button unbuttoned at the neck shows they're specimens of the late 20th century. So is the fact that one is wearing a tie but has it loosened.

In the Fifties there was a lot of talk about The Man in the Gray Flannel Suit. These men worked on Madison Avenue, and gray flannel was their uniform. The young men standing in front of us don't have a uniform. They don't share a style, have no connection with each other. They've inherited clothes, but not a culture. Their culture is picked up on the run.

Today's man isn't a creature of the mind. He is a creature of habit. He hears other people's opinions and adopts them. Ideas rarely if ever figure in his life. He may act for a variety of reasons but seldom from an idea.

You may all sit down now. I don't mean to criticize you. You're young men of your time, and we have to be able to look at you and see that. As actors you must see that we dress the way we think. Nowadays we think in a casual, offhand way, so that's the way we dress.

Now look at the way we sit. How many of us "sit up straight," as we were admonished when we were children? Not many. Mostly we slouch. Our clothes let us do that. You don't wear starched collars the way your great grandfathers did. They didn't slouch. Their clothes saw to that, assuming, of course, that they were middle or upper class.

When we put on the costumes of another time we're not just "dressing up." We're not playing "make believe." We're assuming another way of thinking. We're donning an inheritance, intellectual and spiritual.

You don't think in intellectual or spiritual terms. That's not part of our time, it's why the past is a blank to you. But as an actor you must understand the past clearly enough to bring it to life.

You cannot play *A Streetcar Named Desire* or Paul Green's 1931 play *The House of Connolly*, which is about the decadence of the Southern aristocracy, without knowing the cultural and social position of the South in American history, without knowing, for instance, that in Southern family life there's a fear of mixed blood.

If you're doing Clifford Odets' *Waiting for Lefty* you must have a deep understanding of the Thirties, of the Great Depression. You have to understand labor and unions. Otherwise the play makes no sense.

Odets and Williams and Green are fairly recent writers. Our heritage as actors goes back thousands of years, and we have to feel as comfortable in the clothes, and the language of Sophocles as we do in our sneakers. Think about the clothes and language of Sam Shepard or Lanford Wilson. Sometimes the themes of modern and ancient drama are similar, but not the costumes, nor the idioms.

▼

We've worked on character, studied professions. We've looked into character elements, discovered how much we can get from working with a partner. But the real work begins when you see character in relation to time, which we must begin now.

Start with our own time. If I were to ask these young men to dress up, to "say something" by the way they dress, they'd have come in looking very different, not in blue jeans, not in T-shirts. Very likely they'd have worn jackets and ties. This is a way of acknowledging, perhaps subconsciously, that clothes can give you power.

Your own way of dressing isn't about power. It's about being comfortable, because your comfort takes precedence over everything. I warn you now, if you cling to your comfortable habits, you're contributing to the degradation of the acting profession.

Your dress says, I'm not interested in form. I'm not interested in control. This is what you've lost. The English haven't lost their concern with form and control. The English have a much older, much more uniform culture. Americans have abandoned this along with the rest of the Old World "restraints." This is fine for lounging about the house. Unfortunately one cannot lounge around the stage.

Unlike American life and culture, the stage still requires discipline. You must respect that man has created things for man to wear, that these things have form and they give you power. Naked man has no culture. A man's clothes represent his culture the way a soldier's uniform displays his rank.

Man has created the necktie. Originally it simply held the shirt together at the neck, but it has evolved into an ornament. It has a personality and says something about the man behind it. A necktie is in fact a complicated item to manufacture, and the quality of the materials that go into it, the way it's measured and cut, all say something about the man who wears it. We have to learn to respect the tie and not distort it.

Man has also created the shirt. He was smart enough to put buttons on it. For centuries it was pulled over the head — the button front was a momentous advance. The shirt has its own form, which you must obey. Otherwise you lose whatever power the shirt can give you. If the shirt has been tailored to fit your body closely but your body is bulging out of it, the shirt gives you no power. Quite the contrary — you're playing a clown again. If the shirt isn't tucked into the pants, the shirt loses its power. If the shirt has long sleeves, they should be long. If they're rolled up, you lose power.

Then man created pants, and eventually the zipper. The zipper dictates certain things. It has power over you. But if you accept what it says you can wield its power.

A vital lesson to learn is not to mutilate the form. Your tendency is to say, it's not important. I *have* power. The costume dictates to you *how* to be an actor with power. Pay attention to it. Learn from it. By what you wear and how you wear it you're stating that you're in control. Everything you put on has its definition. Obey it.

On stage you're nothing. You are what the clothes make of you. Clothes say something about your self-control, your self-awareness, your social awareness. Clothes say something about your ability to be restrained, your ability to be respectful. When you wear your own clothes, you're limited to your own mind, your own memory. It's hard to act. You can be only yourself.

I'm very aware that this class is antagonistic to your time. It challenges the suppositions of your time. But you want to be professional, and this is a 2,000-year-old profession.

The professional wears the costume that gives him his character as well as his profession. Would you fight with a policeman? No. By his uniform you know his authority. The policeman, the surgeon, the clergyman wear their uniforms. If not, you'd ignore them. The uniform of the policeman stands for something — law and order. The doctor's lab coat and surgical scrubs represent civilization and healing.

The robes of a judge pass judgment on you before he does. It's not civilized to live without law. That's what the judge stands for. In England the judge wears a white wig. To you this is comical. To the English it is awe-inspiring. If you wear that wig you must find out why, from where it draws its power. These wigs are passed down to succeeding generations of jurists. Some of them are older than America.

When a man puts on a costume he also gives up something of himself, sacrifices something. The policeman in his uniform gives up his personal self for something bigger. The clergyman's costume obliterates the petty self, denies the self in order to serve.

But we live in times when men aren't willing to deny the self. They're not comfortable displaying the authority and power of their professions. They don't want to wear uniforms. Did Jimmy Carter? No. Did Franklin Roosevelt? Yes.

We live in a time and a country where men aren't comfortable with language. The English actor shows he understands form and control by his respect for language. The English actor's language gives him power. We think of all power now as oppressive, as privileged. This is absurd. There's noble power and evil power.

▼

Only man dresses and talks, is civilized. You have to accept responsiblity for civilization, which you do by honoring its symbols. The actor especially must be civilized. He must be a person of self-control. He has to control his body and his costume. He has to control himself in every way.

Learn to respect "things" and their demands. The bed tells us what to do. The chair dictates something else. The chair is made in a certain way. Take the message to heart. You can slide down in the chair, denying its message and end up with a sore back. Try it. Slide down into your chairs. Ruin your posture and your career. Those of you who are less comfortable slouched down may have less far to go. Your mother would be proud. More important, Sophocles would be proud.

Each "thing" is made for a purpose. Respect it. Learn its demands. It's a way of knowing and respecting civilization, what man has made. There's something corrupted about the way you treat life and mistreat things. To you a catchphrase for "things" is "shit." "Look at all this shit I brought," you say. *Everything* to you is shit. And you're the one stuck in it. Every "thing" has its history, its life, its demands, its reason for respect.

Learn to respect the spaces man has made. Space dictates to you, teaches you control. Being in a church affects your dress. It affects how you behave. You've grown up in a world that's told you "you" are everything. On the stage "you" are nothing. You only matter when you're a character in circumstances.

The way we behave is dictated by circumstances. Would you say, in a sloppy way, "Hi!" to the pope? To Stella? No. That much of history is still in you, restrains you. You have to recover a greater sense of what being human is — formal, eternal, controlled.

▼

I began by saying we must understand character in relation to time. Let's once again start with nature. We can always learn from nature. Let's turn on the projector and start with a slide of some tall trees. Trees grow up, up, up, trying to reach the sky. This natural upward movement reaches out to the sky but also yields to natural forces.

Stand up. Let your body grow tall. Stretch your arms up, up, up. Reach for the sky. Now imagine yourself buffetted by winds. Sway to the right, the left, forward, backward, but gracefully, bending only slightly. The tree yields. Get an impression of giving in, of yielding from the tree.

Next a slide of a huge rock. Like the tree, the rock is deeply rooted. Unlike the tree, the rock doesn't yield. Nothing affects the rock, no matter what you do around it. The rock is immovable. It can't go forward, can't go backward. It's not easily conquered by the environment. It can be broken, sheered by the wind, but not destroyed.

Its strength as a rock comes from a solid base. Power comes from rootedness. That's our whole trouble. We're uprooted. That's where we differ from the old actors. They knew they had a base and could be strong on top. This is the rock's influence on man. Man needs power. He needs a base to provide that power.

Let's stand and be that rock. A man's power can be rooted by standing like a rock. You have to emanate strength. Let's see that the whole body's a rock — the head, the neck, the eyes. A rock never loses its base. It can be splintered, but it remains a rock. Unlike the tree, which yields, the rock splits the wind.

The next slide shows the ruins of a Greek temple. Here's our first introduction to what man has done with the rock. In the Greek temples man created form. He's in control of nature through design and repetition. That is power. In our time we have destroyed form and are formless ourselves.

Man announced himself by creating his world. He took something that was there, the rock, and gave it form. He trimmed the rock. He shaped it. And he repeated it. He created a sense of continuity and order. He intended it to last for thousands of years.

The next slide is a closeup of a Greek column. The Greek contribution was to turn rock into sculpture. The columns are fluted. The capitals are sculpted. None of this diminishes the strength of the rock. Even in a temple in ruins, the strength of its rock endures.

The Greeks transformed rocks into a human creation. The rock became organized, sculpted. The pillars are lined up, symmetrical, in perfect balance. Man deals with the strength of the rock creatively but also makes it a symbol of order. Nothing about the pillar is wild.

Man takes the power of marble and adds form, design, decoration. Without a strong base you can't have the decoration. Without a base you can't decorate yourself. The sculptor takes rock and articulates it. You need that base, that strength to define behavior, expression, words. In creating form man is at *his* strongest.

The columns have crowns and capitals on them. Man has articulated the base, then he tops it off with his own symbol of power, the crown. You decorate yourself to show that you're a man with certain power. We have lost the kingdom because we've lost the decorative form. Man must wear the symbol of his power — the crown, or the business suit.

▼

I want you all to come on stage. Stand in a way that expresses the power that comes from the ground up. Say, "I feel that power, coming up through the earth into me."

Now form a circle as if you were the base of a pillar, the intervals between you regular, even. Look at the people on either side. You're strong because you're duplicated and repeated. Be conscious of the form you're creating. I don't want you scattered randomly.

All right, now start moving, but keep the strength of the

base. Keep the sense of order. As you move, stand tall. Now I want you to be formless. I want to see you slouch, to cave in, to droop. Do this just for a minute. Now regain your form as a pillar. Man has conquered formlessness. He's now in control of himself. He recognizes the form in himself and in the next person.

Now let's look at a medieval cathedral. It uses the same basic formula. It has repetition. It has symmetry. It implies continuity. It radiates power. There isn't a piece of stone on the cathedral that isn't decorated. Decoration and power go together.

As actors, we have to learn to dress in a way that gives us power. The tendency today is to dress as if we're garbage. You must change your idea of what the human being is — you have to see him as formal, eternal, controlled. As actors, if you act without this power, if you're unable to use it, you're like the leaves clustered helplessly around the base of the pillars.

Something deep in man requires decorating. He doesn't walk naked in the street. We're losing this sense of decoration for power; if we lose it all, we'll have lost the sense of survival. We're unstructured at this moment in our society. The structure we're looking at, the church, isn't naked. It's designed. When you clothe yourself, you've designed yourself, like the cathedral.

Today you're oriented toward fashion, not design or style. Fashion merely exploits. It's not about power, but only about surface decoration. We're strong enough to have built cathedrals. We have the strength to reach up, like the cathedral, to some larger self. The power is in you. Call it, or don't call it God. This is where the cathedral has drawn much of its decorations and its power, the something we all still understand at heart. But let the outside reflect what's inside, something powerful, not slovenly or broken.

You must have a sense that form creates character, that character grows from a strong base. Two of the Greek gods illustrated their understanding of civilization, one in the negative sense, that is the absence of civility, and one in the positive sense. They had Dionysus, the god of wine and fun, and Apollo, who represented the civilized side of man. Dionysus glorifies erotic love in all its madness and fury. Apollo represented spiritual love, the love that ennobles, helps others. Today we still have Dionysus, the party animal, but we have driven Apollo from our Olympus. He's too square.

Civilization, however, means you don't indulge or allow yourself to do anything you want. Civilization *means* restraint and control. There's no easier way to see the meaning of civilization than to study the medieval clergy.

For next class I want you to come in the costume of the clergy. For a nun or a priest in the medieval Catholic church the costume is the character. What you put on is the character. What you put on affects you inside.

Prepare some gestures that go with that costume and bring in a passage from the King James Bible, not a modern translation, to give us in costume. It may not improve your souls, but it will improve your acting.

CHAPTER SEVENTEEN

LEARNING A CHARACTER'S RHYTHM

Today I see I have a room full of nuns and bishops and monks and abbesses. Let's have one of the nuns on stage. There was a moment in history when mankind found a form — through the church — that allowed him to give up everything pleasurable, everything desirable, everything instinctive in him — in order to produce purity, love, communication.

Look at the whiteness of our nun's habit. The flowing drape hides all womanly beauty. Her hair, her breasts, everything physically attractive, is concealed. Virtually all we can see apart from her face is her "sensible shoes."

The clergy dresses the way the church thinks. The church understands the nature of sacrifice. When we looked at the Greek columns we saw a strong solid base. We felt the root strength. We should feel the same in those who wear the costumes of a religious order. The members of an order are like columns. They dress exactly alike. They're not representatives of individuality. Their repetition gives a sense of belonging.

They *share* a way of thinking. We, on the contrary, are *alone* in our way of thinking. We're left out. Each of us is by ourself. Those of us in this room share only one thing, our commitment to the theatre. We share our commonness as actors. But we have no way of wearing it. If we belong to a religious order what we wear proclaims our commitment to God, our aching need to serve God. For most of you this is a very foreign way of thinking. The cosmic value has gone out of you. Materialism is all you've known. The advertisers, after all, don't want their good customers disappearing into monasteries and nunneries!

Now I'd like our young nun in white to sit on the stage. That's right. Cross your legs. Take one shoe off. Rumple your stocking. Lean backward with your weight on your elbow. Are you comfortable sitting like that? Of course not. The costume made you want to sit up.

I have you sitting like a tramp, not a nun. It goes against the costume and against the character.

Now you see the costume *is* the character. What you put on is the character, affects you inside. What's outside makes you feel certain things inside. The costume helps us conquer our impulse to slop about and be comfortable.

▼

In looking at the world the Greeks created we saw that civilization meant you can't indulge yourself or just do anything you want. Civilization means restraint and control.

In the Renaissance painters exalted the Madonna and her child. You can't have a more exquisite portrait of restraint than these Madonnas. Their expressions are full of tenderness. All their love is being given away. It goes out to the world in the deepest sense. "Me" is hidden in these Madonnas. All of me, they're saying, is hidden to give everything to you.

The love in these paintings is gentler than any you're used to seeing depicted. Your sense of love is too angular, too muscular. The love of the Madonna flows from the heart out to the world. Yours flows from the world into your pockets.

The clergy are symbols of civilization. Nuns are clothed

either in white or in black. They show no hair, wear no orna-
ments — only the cross.

The symbol of the priest is the clerical collar. It is the symbol of being civilized. Everything about the priest is in order.

For the priest or the nun the body is covered, hidden. The
priest's costume helps him deny the pleasures of the layman. It
helps him quiet and perhaps even kill the instinct for stealing,
dope, sex. You must sacrifice everything to serve civilization
through the church. The costume hides your baser self, frees
you to give to others. You also gain a strength at the root. You
have no fear, no hesitation when you feel you are doing something in the service of God.

You must understand that each character has a rhythm. In
the church the rhythm is peace and quiet. A nun doesn't need to
hurry. She's secure in her circumstances. You learn this from the
costume — it teaches you how to walk.

▼

Let's all get up on the stage and get into lines of five. Make
sure to leave the exact same space between each of you and
between the rows. We're working for the sameness that gives us
strength. I'm going to ring a bell, at which you'll do a gesture of
the clergy — kneeling, praying, crossing yourself.

Each of you is doing something different. It doesn't give you
a feeling of strength, does it?

This time when I ring the bell, all kneel together. The second time I ring, cross yourselves. The third time you'll sing
Kyrie Eleison — Lord, have mercy on us — in unison as you
cross yourselves.

Very good. Now go back to your seats — in character! Don't
disintegrate into individuals.

This exercise should help you understand that civilization

develops forms to relate man to the world. In the church's forms you lose yourself to find the world. This isn't something animals do. But man has made himself recognize the world. He has created words for it. Man alone dresses and talks.

Man recognizes he is responsible for civilization. You must understand you break civilization when you don't recognize its symbols. The actor must be civilized, must be a person of self-control. He must control his body — in costume, but also control himself in every way.

Restrictions of the body make gestures restricted. If your hands were chained together, you could move them only so much. If you were a prisoner you would resent this constraint. But if you are a person of the cloth you accept the restriction. You see it as an invitation to acquiescence. You know there's a greater strength in acquiescence than impotent rage.

Actors have to avoid the conventional, the inherited cliché. The life of restriction isn't sad, though it may have sadness in it. It has its own joy. You have to find the joy (as well as the sadness). A child is born to the world. That gives you joy. So does the thought that you serve God, which makes you part of the world. You have to feel the uplifting sense of joy and security. You have to understand the pleasure of giving. It creates security, peace, health. And it makes others civilized.

▼

Let me have four volunteers. Sit on the stage facing each other. Even when you sit I want to see a sense of your power. In every movement I want to sense you reaching up, like the cathedral, to some larger power. You must always remember we're strong enough to build cathedrals. Say to yourself, "I am powerful, not slovenly or broken."

Now discuss whether the clergy should be permitted to marry. This is a big idea. I want you to think before you say anything. But be restrained by the costumes. Make your points by the power of the idea.

Be very careful of gestures. Thinking restrains gestures. Extraneous gestures get in the way of ideas. In this circumstance spontaneous gestures are unnecessary. Our jerky, meaningless gestures need restraint. Gestures don't have to be as ignorant as ours usually are.

If you use gesture, it must be flowing, extended. They can't be personal gestures, which lack the anatomy of thought. They have to be in the nature of a wave, a curve, nothing rigid.

I don't want to see any "self" in the argument. It's not about what "I" think. The ideas must have the authority of an institution, must have size. Trying to understand the thinking of the church is a good exercise for you because you must learn not to be ordinary. You're here to have your talent aroused. But first you must cure the disorder in your soul.

Our lives must have order. The sun goes up, it goes down. We live, we die. There are patterns in life. There are no kids in the theatre, only men and ideas. Child actors on stage must be controlled, animals too, but an actor controls himself.

You should want to act only because you want to be led to something bigger in life. You should know that life will be dreary and your acting even drearier until you learn to give something away. That's why these exercises are useful. They're not just about learning to play a certain character. They're about the world itself.

(The actors discuss whether the clergy should marry.)

All right, that's a start. You must see by now that these exercises are not something you do once, then forget about. They're not another part of your disposable culture. They can continue teaching you as long as you're willing to work on them.

When you play a clergyman you're part of a society in which

words have size, a society that speaks. You're part of an order with a duty to deliver a message. Don't bring it down to the meanness of everything else in your life. If you can only soil it, then please just leave it be.

Think of your selections from the King James Bible. The words in this translation were chosen for their beauty and meaning. Don't turn them into "natural" prose. If you do you're pulling down the whole American Theatre for a childish prank. To amuse yourself alone. While impoverishing everyone else. Please, just play some other game somewhere else. Don't mock institutions and ideas that have stood the test of time.

▼

Who'd like to read us his Bible passage? I'm asking you to do something you've been prepared for. You know how to build circumstances. You have to decide whom you're addressing. The need to speak these words must come from the outside. Are you reading the Bible to a group of nuns? What will they expect of you? To a group of children? The child wants you to explain, to teach, to forgive.

Part of your preparation of these texts is to see images behind them. If you're reading the 23rd Psalm you must have an image behind "green pastures" or we'll say, "We've heard that!" That's simply bad preaching.

You also must justify what you're doing. Decide where you're speaking. Is it a classroom? A room in a monastery? From the pulpit? To whom are you speaking? A room full of monks? a child who's sinned? Are you at the side of a grave? Before the high altar?

More than many of the things we're required to do, playing a religious character demands a special relationship to words. I've often said the script is in you, not just in the author's words. The author's words are lifeless without the meaning you bring to them. But when you deal with a Biblical text, or, for that matter, Shakespeare, the words do have a special life.

And it's this: If you're a nun or a priest you know that you have the strength, the power, the authority of God in you! You know what God says. As a nun, you're able to meet every situation, understand it and find a solution for it. "Problems" aren't so overwhelming. You understand things like chastity and death. You're secure in the words of God.

When you speak as a nun we must see that you don't struggle. We must know that you know. You know about man and his corruption. You have God in you. That gives you authority! You minister the soul of the world. You represent God's knowledge. Don't be humble. God speaks through you.

You're God's child, not a street kid. The costume gives you the power of God. You must understand the size of Divine Authority.

This is a case where the words matter more than the feeling. Let the words do it. Don't "feel" too much. Don't let "feeling" overwhelm the words. We want to hear the words more than the emotion.

Get pleasure from the language. If you don't, you change the style. Get a sense of power from those words. Link the thoughts and the language, so that we get a rhythm. Be loud but not angry.

An excellent piece for you to work on now is Isabella's speech to her brother in *Measure for Measure*.

O you beast!
O faithless coward! O dishonest wretch!
Wilt thou be made a man out of my vice?
Is't not a kind of incest, to take life
From thine own sister's shame? What should I think?
Heaven shield my mother play'd my father fair!
For such a warped slip of wilderness

Ne'er issued from his blood. Take my defiance!
Die, perish! Might but my bending down
Reprieve thee from thy fate, it should proceed:
I'll pray a thousand prayers for thy death,
No word to save thee.
Thy sin's not accidental, but a trade.
Mercy to thee would prove itself a bawd:
'Tis best that thou diest quickly.

Isabella is urging her brother to die so she can preserve her virginity. I can't think of any idea more foreign to the way you think. Apart from the language's beauty, her plea will tell you what it means to be governed by ideas, not feelings.

Isabella is thinking big ideas. Her ideas are more important to her than what she "feels." She's urging her brother to die to keep her clean for the world. To do that she must believe her mission in the world is far more important than his life.

This is not to say she doesn't love him. But she knows that there is a greater love than the one that binds human beings together. She is imploring him on behalf of a far more profound love. She can only ask him to make this sacrifice because their love for each other is clear but she is also relying on his ability to see that her commitment to the religious life, her ability to help the world as a nun transcends the value of either of their lives.

That's bigger than the A&P.

ACTORS ARE ARISTOCRATS

Nine-tenths of acting is the obligations of the student. By now I hope you've given up the idea that "she'll tell me." You're not here just to listen to me and write things down. That's not learning. You're here to learn to stretch yourself in life, and in so doing on stage as well.

This class is intended to help you get away from yourselves, from your banal understanding of language and, perhaps most of all, from your democratized mind. I have often told you that you believe as Americans that your society is classless. That isn't true. The classes don't conform to classical European conventions, but they exist.

As actors we have to transcend the class structure. We're workers, but not working class. We're generally from middle-class families, but we have to free ourselves from the prejudices and conventions of the middle-class mind. We're sometimes from the wealthy classes, but we can't be confined to their mindset.

If anything we should identify ourselves with the aristocracy. There is no aristocratic class in America. There are very wealthy people who have behaved like aristocrats but generally only in expenditures. They have the money part, but not the class. They don't have the true freedom, the spacious mind, the deep esthetic sense of the aristocrat.

We've studied the clergy in its purest form, the clergy of the Middle Ages, when religion dominated the Western world. The clergymen you're likely to play will seldom conform to the models we've been studying, but these are the ideals from which the latter-day clergy descend.

To understand in the fullest sense what a priest or a nun can be, and once was, is a great help in understanding a modern clergyman. It's extremely useful to see how the modern mentality inhibits the clergyman from realizing the role he fulfilled in the Middle Ages. The modern clergyman is, by contrast to his medieval forebear, broken. The sense of what the modern world has broken is extremely important to us as actors.

▼

We're now going to study the aristocratic class, which has also been disinherited by the modern world. The aristocratic class once played a decisive role in the world. There are times it still can play this role. When the United Nations celebrated the 50th anniversary of its founding, royalty were invited, and their presence, their authority were unmistakable.

We are going to study the aristocrat at his purest, when he dominated the world, when the world accepted his right to dominate them. The banishment of the ruling class has helped the masses but hurt the theatre.

One of our weaknesses as American actors is the lack of tradition, of order. Behind the English actor is the crown. Prince Charles has the crown and the aristocratic mind. Edward VIII had to give up his crown. The English have a sense of something to give up or to hold up. For the most part, we don't. The U.S. Senate has traditions. Senators dress for their profession. They don't slouch about.

But the American actor has no tradition. He slouches. He doesn't dress. Thanks to television. Television wants you as yourself. The acting profession doesn't want *you*. Only what you can make of yourself. English actors know this.

Actors must develop a sense of history, a realization that everything has a historical base. We worked on this a little at the very beginning of the technique when we were putting the red, white and blue objects into their contexts, to see a certain shade of red as the red of a certain time. To see that what surrounded that shade of red also spoke of a certain time.

You don't value intimacy with objects. That also is very much a mentality of today. You see an object, you use it, and you throw it away. It took civilization to create the clock. It took thousands of years of civilization to understand a piece of paper.

In the current social moment that sense of the past is absent. Kleenex is a substitute for a handkerchief. A piece of Kleenex is white, neat, orderly, but it has its moment, gets used up and is thrown away. This is true of most of our culture. A paper cup is brilliantly designed. It's useful. The whole world can use it. But it won't last. It will be used up and thrown away. We live in a disposable culture where there's no way you can keep most things. They must give way so that the next may be purchased, the faster the better.

By contrast, the aristocratic mind has a sense of continuity. The aristocrat lives in a world whose things have been preserved for centuries. He lives in a world where durability is prized — and beauty.

That sense of time is important to us as actors. The aristocrat, until a few centuries ago, wasn't worried about income. He was concerned with his rights, his duties and his pleasures. We as actors don't have this luxury. While it's very difficult for actors to make a living, the last thing I want you to take from this class is that the actor is just an ignorant person trying to make a buck.

Like the aristocrat, the actor lives in ideas. Ideas are what playwrights write about. If you speak ideas, they enter into you. They become yours. Accumulating ideas is what gives you power.

You must have minds capable of such ideas. History has created the Aristocratic Mind, which can convey its thoughts to the whole world. That's the tradition to which you as actors belong.

▼

I have stressed from the beginning that you must not speak commonly. You must lose the common tone most of you brought here. It's too fast for us to understand the words. Too modern, too ignorant. There's insufficient dignity, nor enough self-possession or courage.

Your way of speaking is dull, because you don't understand how to make sense verbally to your partner. You don't speak to his mind. You don't *strive* to make sense. You tend to let it all drop to the floor. More refuse.

From the minute you stand up to work we must sense you intend to take everybody with you. Too often I sense in your attitude you're mad at the world, so you exclude it. You walk with loneliness and abandonment, as if to say, "Oh, well, I'm nothing." Get over that.

Have confidence in yourself. Don't feel it's your destiny to be more refuse: Free yourself! You must feel you're worthy of bigger-than-life ideas. You must have a nobility of mind, a sense of your own power. You must have a stronger sense of who you are than television does. Television gives you a passive image. Its whole purpose is to pacify, not to engage. If you think you're only a docile consumer, you'll sink, sink, sink! You must believe you deserve to dress and think like aristocrats. You wear a crown, not a baseball cap. No one ever disposes of a crown.

Say to me, "I swear to you, Stella, that I'll achieve the size God has given me as an actor. No more pizzi-caca!"

▼

As an aristocrat you understand the tradition of handing down. Do you have something handed down from your grandmother? If so, you understand that what is handed down is respected and cherished. In the case of an aristocrat, what's handed down is social position, a sense of esthetics and morality. From what's handed down you derive a sense that you're not alone. You always have your inheritance.

That sense of an ongoing tradition should underline the way you speak as an actor. You have to give each important word its full, unique value. You have to give up your sense that you have a right to speak in your personal, wobbly rhythm. You're a person of tradition. Don't speak without a sense of your inheritance. Don't lose your 2,000-year inheritance of strength and power, no matter what. Don't let TV buy you.

We have to rise above our disposable time. Look at that piano in the corner. It's an upright. It was designed and built very carefully decades and decades ago. It's a musical instrument, but it's been used, really used. It's lost its quality. The keys are beginning to go. The sound is tinny. Gradually it will be thrown out. Its moment is over. It's too expensive to repair. So it gets thrown out.

I asked if you had things you received from your grandmothers. Maybe it was a perfume bottle with a stopper. You keep it for its sentimental value. You don't keep perfume in it. It's not practical. You don't keep it for its practicality. It's decoration. Handing down a perfume bottle is essentially a very old-fashioned idea. To think it will last is an illusion. If you give it to your daughter she'll eventually give it or throw it away because its usefulness is over. Your grandchildren will have atomizers. They won't even know what a stopper is. But they won't know what tradition is either.

We're not interested in useless things, though we grudgingly acknowledge decoration as a kind of use. We don't build castles any more. We build high-rises. Castles have no heat, no running water. They're not practical. What do we need them for? They're purely decoration. So is the Cunard steamship line. Jets are much faster and to the point.

We live in a time when even countries are used up, ways of life are used up. In our century there's a whole literature that deals with time and transition. Chekhov gives you a sense of transition in a country that had nobility. It had a czar, a gentry. Chekhov's plays show you some aristocrats of the mind — with a decaying land and culture. He's showing you what is going to burn out.

In Chekhov's plays we witness for the first time the working man on stage with an accurate understanding of the working man's position. Even when he's "in his place" Chekhov's working man has much more power than the cultured gentry with their aristocratic minds.

Tennessee Williams was greatly influenced by Chekhov. A Williams play always has some aristocrat going under.

There was a time, of course, when the clergyman was going under and the aristocrat was taking his place. For many hundreds of years the church was the dominant power. It used its power to submerge the individual.

The philosophy of the church also denied individual expression. It exalted the poor, the frail, the dying, the unhappy. It ordered people to be humble, that they must give to, serve and bless God. But its high ideals also became corrupted. The costume became a false mark, a shield, not a true symbol.

One of the first ideas of the aristocratic mind is that the body isn't to be covered up, not submerged. The body is to be celebrated. This too they got from the Greek ideal. The aristocratic man supposes a strong physique, blooming, full and abundant. The aristocratic man symbolizes exuberant health. The maintenance of that health implies war, adventure, hunting, games, tournaments — everything that embraces strong, free and cheerful actions.

Every social class, every tradition has those who don't live up, who are phonies. The aristocracy has had its tyrants, the church its hypocrites and Inquisitors. Concentrate rather on the nobility of the ideal. Take what is good from tradition, not what is unfilfilled.

Good, strong, noble, beautiful, happy, "favored by God" — these were the aristocratic virtues.

▼

The Greek nobility described the lower classes with pity and indulgence. This attitude was handed down. The well-born didn't have to create their happiness superficially by lording it over their enemies, their inferiors, as resentful people do. Likewise, they knew, being strong, active people, that happiness is inseparable from action. This was a different kind of happiness from that of the oppressed. In the oppressed were feelings of hostility. It appears as a need. It's a narcotic, a drug. It's there even when it apppears to be covered by peace and calm.

The true, noble aristocrat lives with confidence and openness. The resentful man is neither sincere nor honest nor straightforward. His mind loves hiding places, secret paths and back doors. Everything hidden impresses him as his security, his comfort. He knows waiting. He knows self-deprecation, self-humiliation. A race of such resentful men in the end will, of necessity, supplant the aristocratic race. Their cunning and deceit will win out. They're survivors, not creators. But what kind of life do they bequeath?

A certain thoughtlessness, a brave recklessness in the face of danger, all that enthusiastic suddenness of anger, love, awe gratitude, vengeance have been noted in the aristocratic spirit.

As for resentfulness, the aristocrat has it but expends it in immediate action, so it doesn't poison him. Unfailingly, the resentment poisons the weak and impotent. The aristocrat sees the misdeeds of his enemy but doesn't take them seriously. This is the sign of a strong, full nature. Such a man simply shakes off adversity where another would suffer. A nobleman has respect for his foe — and such respect is a bridge to love. The aristocrat couldn't have an enemy unless he honored him.

The leveling down of the European man is our greatest danger. This is the prospect that depresses us. Today we see nothing that wants to become greater. We suspect that all goes ever downward, becoming thinner, more sleazy, smarter, cozier, more ordinary, more indifferent. Exactly here lies our crisis. With the fear of man, we have also lost the love of man — reverence for him, hope in him. The human prospect wearies us. What is the current nihilism if it is not that? We are tired of man.

As actors we have to build a renewed sense that man *has* power and beauty, that noble man is not buried in a democratized mob. We must learn to separate politics from culture, from character. We must be aristocrats in a world of noble equals. We must find and keep the best of both worlds, the old and the new.

As American actors we don't have the inner majesty and understanding that the English have. They have it because they have the crown, which gives them the sense, "I am an actor." We are socially democratized. We don't know who we are.

Actors are aristocrats of the mind! And have been for well over 2,000 years!

For next class come in dressed as aristocrats. The aristocrat assumes the right to decorate himself. That's also the heritage of the actor. I want you to "decorate" yourself and come in prepared to say, "I deserve that."

MAKING THE COSTUME REAL

Character is physicalization — with truth. I'll even let you write that down. Everything you say, everything you do defines your character. The outside is what counts most in character. Your physical self is the most interesting thing in character.

Take your walk. Most of you, when you walk, are saying, "I'm young. I'm good looking. I'm stupid. Help me, somebody." But when you play a character your costume should help you change your walk.

Because you're in costume today many of you are sitting with more dignity than usual. Most of the time you sit there, legs apart, slouched, comfortable. Would you sit that way in front of the president? Well, you shouldn't, even if you would. Would you like me to sit like that, and teach? No. This is hard for a late 20th century actor who wants to play character. But you must understand your heritage. What you're working with isn't just something you find in the street.

Your costumes are splendid. They should help you understand the thinking of anybody in a class society. The people who dress this way have Oxford and Cambridge behind them. It's not the costume but the mind that's important. The social status gave them the right to dress like that.

In a society that has an aristocracy the costume is a thing of value. Like real diamonds. It says, "Look! Look!" There's value in a thing made beautifully, that has form. People are aware their clothes are saying something about their minds. The Queen of England's jewelry is kept very carefully. Her crown is in the Tower of London under heavy guard. Her crown isn't just an object. It's rarely even used as an actual piece of clothing. It's mostly an idea.

It's important that you feel secure in these costumes. You must be in absolute control, certain that nothing will fall off. Also, with such costumes a little makeup would help. Do something to extend your eyes, darling, to get away from that bare, democratized face.

With you dressed this way, this shouldn't be an acting class. It should be an opportunity to *live* in this class, to think with an aristocratic mind. Aristocracy forces you to deal with ideas, not words, not feelings.

The aristocrat is concerned with clarity. That was the aristocrat's great advance over the church. After centuries of living in darkness and mysticism, man wanted clarity and understanding. That's why the aristocracy triumphed over the church.

The church emphasized the overwhelming nothingness of man. The aristocratic mind had a new sense of man — as ruler, as citizen, as artist. All this led to what we call the Renaissance man, which was a rebirth of classical man.

The aristocratic man is in pursuit of an articulate, creative self. He sees himself as an individual, not as part of a mass. He wants to beautify himself, not just the church. He wants power. He wants to be knowledgeable.

▼

I'd like you to stand up in your costumes. It can't be the weary, defensive, slouching way you normally stand. When you're an aristocrat even standing is a mode of self-assertion, self-affirmation.

Your costume must feed you. Be careful of regarding your costume as "make believe." You mustn't lie to your body. If you do, you kill your talent. What you put on is going to be part of you. Live in it. Marry it. Don't cheapen yourself by cheapening your costume. Learn to change your outside. Become the character. Have the inner dignity to do this work for yourself.

In the way you've costumed yourselves you've understood the aristocratic love of beauty. That's because the aristocrat, as a result of his education, surrounds himself with the best of everything. The costume is the revelation that you understand power and its responsibility. Your duty as an aristocrat is to maintain, to uphold, to reveal the society's finest standards.

You reveal this not only in dress but also in gesture. The way you gesture must be refined, controlled. You must reach the point where you *need* to make a gesture — then restrain it. See what gestures you need. Then give it no more, no less than it needs. Otherwise it will be casual, contemporary, cluttered.

All this modern, contemporary gesturing is perfectly all right because we have nothing to say. When you have something to say, you need control.

You must be able to take every class into yourself — that's what makes you an actor. Be like the musician with a violin. The music comes from the violin. Take care of it, protect it.

As an aristocrat you have to learn to enjoy power. Power enabled the aristocrat to believe in such things as poetry, music, beauty. With aristocratic man comes a sense that art is something worthwhile.

Art and power gave people another sense of life, totally different from what the church had given them. Man could avail himself of that power and say, "I'm a man! I'll put the cloak on me! Everything around me will be big and beautiful. It will represent the way man wants to live." The king will live surrounded by authority, power, art and majesty. He made the church of secondary value.

The king took on the duty to rule. He understood that this

meant he needed to know history, math, architecture, painting, music, philosophy. Along with the aristocracy comes the idea of the importance of education. If Prince Charles is invited to speak at the 350th anniversary of the founding of Harvard, it is because he is an extremely well educated man. He has the right to speak at Harvard.

The aristocrat represents man in pursuit of an articulate, creative self. He sees himself as an individual. He wants to beautify himself and his world as well as the church.

The impressions and principles of the aristocratic mind aren't abstractions. They've been made visible in architecture. You can see them in this slide of the exterior of Versailles. This is where Louis XIV lived! It answers the question, "How should a man of power live?" Everything around him must be beautified.

The space must be controlled as precisely as mathematics is controlled. The architecture is controlled. The gardens are controlled. So are the paths, the sculpture, everything. The palace, like Louis XIV, is in complete control. The design *is* control.

This next slide is of the palace's Hall of Mirrors. In the court of Louis XIV man became an individual who lived with the advantage of culture all around him. It was no longer the church but the power of a single individual who ruled the country. That was why everything that surrounded him needed to express control.

The intention of the architecture is control, but that doesn't mean it's exclusively authoritarian. The architecture reflects an ecstatic love of beauty. Not one inch of that room is left bare. From here there's no possible way of going back to darkness.

Here there's room for the rhythm of the artist's hand. The man who made the chandelier had a craft. He was aware of the importance of the other crafts. He wanted to be part of the painting, the sculpture, the architecture.

With the ascendance of the aristocratic mind, the artist also gained power. The artist became what the king and the people revered and admired. The artist says, "With my co-workers I create light, beauty and form." The artist today no longer has that feeling, that power. The mechanized world has taken the art out of man.

Let's look one more time at a church interior. It's beautiful. It's hauntingly beautiful. It's dark, symmetrical, but what it says is that man must give himself up. He must give up his "self." He must not worry about personal happiness or personal evaluation.

Now we're back in Versailles. Could the contrast be more dramatic? Here space is used to create beauty. Here everything is light and polished. We know the names of the artists who created these rooms. They have a part in a moment of history, unlike the artists and artisans of the Middle Ages, who sacrificed their identities for the greater glory of God.

Everything in this room was made by hand. It was created by artists. Nothing was "manufactured." Everything is decorated, draped, designed. All the basic building elements are turned into works of art.

The new man takes a piece of wood and says, "Wood will be used so that it becomes a work of art." He makes a desk for Louis XIV. The desk is a symbol of order, design and beauty. The new man takes ordinary things — spoons, salt cellars, coffee pots — and makes them in silver and gold. He turns everything he touches into art.

The new man sculpts staircase bannisters and chandeliers with nude women. The clergy covered the body. The new man says, "The body is beautiful. It can be uncovered. It can be draped. It can be shown off."

You can't come into this room and sit on the floor. That's not what the carpet was created for.

The clergy declared that the earth belonged to God. Everything belonged to God including himself. The new man decorated himself the way the clergy decorated the altar. He knew he was worthy of it. Everything the king wore was designed, controlled and beautiful — his walking stick, his shoes, his cape, his wig. He wasn't ashamed to reveal his legs. Everything he put on, everything he saw was designed to give him power, glory, dignity.

Here's a slide of Elizabeth the First. She's decorated from head to foot. Her hair is teased, curled, jeweled. Look at the great beauty of her sleeves. What she's put on is great art and gives her power.

Here, a few centuries later, are a nobleman and his wife, painted by Gainsborough. Looking at the painting, you have the sense they belong to themselves. They wear plumes, ribbons, gloves, grand hats. They have worked to decorate themselves but feel entirely secure in it. When we play aristocrats we need this confidence, this security.

In the middle of the 19th century Queen Victoria visited Paris. She and Prince Albert went to the Paris Opera with Napoleon III, who gave himself the title Emperor, and his wife, the "Empress" Eugenie.

The Parisians, who have always had the snobbish ability to understand the meaning of every little gesture, noticed that when the monarchs seated themselves Eugenie, just for a second, looked behind her to see if the servant was pushing the chair under her. Victoria sat down without breaking her forward gaze. There wasn't a flicker of doubt in her mind that her chair would be exactly where it ought.

▼

To physicalize the aristocratic mind the first thing we must insist on is formality. Even in relating to your partners as aristocrats there must be a certain space between you. You can't have the American, casual, mindless intimacy. You can't have that instinctive giving in to spontaneous gestures. These people never allow themselves to be seen informally. You never see a king leaning on a table. These people require a certain space.

As you get up to work don't walk without going somewhere. Most of you, when you walk, I think to myself, "I walk like that when they tell me I must walk for my health and I have no real destination." You must walk in style with a clear sense of where you want to go. You're going into circumstances, not just the center of the classroom or onto the stage. Into circumstances!

When you walk in these costumes we must sense classical antiquity and its noble understanding of man talking. We must sense you live not in a mundane world but one where things that last forever, where philosophical ideas matter, where words matter more than "feelings."

The aristocrat knows he's someone. Most of you can't say, "I *am someone*." You think you've never been someone, and the truth is that many of you are perfectly happy to be nobody. If you learn to be an actor you can never be "nobody," because you'll be able to make ideas clear, and if you can do that you *are somebody*.

I know all this is hard for Americans, because you've been brought up to be ashamed of self-importance.

▼

Each of you take a partner. I'm going to put on a record so you can waltz. To understand the aristocratic mentality we should really work on the minuet, but I'm assuming none of us knows the minuet and I hope everyone knows how to do the waltz. All right, I'll start the record and you waltz around the stage.

Your costumes help you with the form, don't they? You're holding each other but you have to keep a certain distance. Your arms have to achieve a certain form. You don't hold each other in the waltz as you do in the fox trot. The fox trot is more relaxed. You hold each other more intimately. When the waltz first came in it was considered scandalous. It was so fast, so intoxicating. But now the waltz is about elegance. The costumes and the movements help. They give you "presence."

All right, let's stop for a minute. Just for a second do one of the dances that's fashionable right now? Fine. That's ugly. It doesn't work in these costumes, does it? It looks ridiculous. Of course, it looks ridiculous in any clothes. Do the people have a relationship to each other other than an animal or mechanical one? Do they have form? Do they have elegance? Do they have "presence?" No. Today we even dance like machines. Robots in heat.

Let's return to the waltz. I'll start the record again. Very good. Keep the rhythm — *one*, two three, *one* two three. Do you find that keeping the rhythm inhibits you? No. It's a form of restraint, but emphasizing the rhythm adds to the joyfulness of the dance. Give yourself to the rhythm of the music. You're not accustomed to moving to a rhythm, you've never known the pleasure.

Let's have six men and six women walk up on stage and line up, the men in one line, the women in the other. First bow to each other. As you bow, reveal your adornments, which is a way of revealing your power.

Now I want the men to imagine they're noblemen and the women they're bowing to the queen. I want to sense you're acknowledging greater power, acknowledging *someone*. You don't have to lose your aristocratic self to do so.

Do you understand why bowing is more potent than shaking hands? Why the Japanese still bow? It gives their greetings a deeper sense of nuance.

Now, women, offer your hands to be kissed, and men, bow to kiss the ladies' hands. In this case the kiss is just a brush of the lips.

Now I need someone to be king. You'll do just fine. First the women approach their monarch and bow. It must be graceful, sincere, dignified, deeply respectful but without any loss of your own aristocratic self.

Now I want the king to go into the wings. The rest of you start conversing. I want the king to make an entrance with enough presence that you are immediately aware of him and hush.

Then arrange yourselves in a line. As he passes you, bow to him and show him something very special that you are wearing. Justify its importance.

You may return to your seats — but again, without losing your aristocratic manner. As you sit you are not just taking your places in class. Let's have a sense you're ascending the throne.

Next to costumes nothing feeds the imagination as much as gestures. "For God's sake," you're thinking. "Do I have to worry about gesture too?" Yes, you do!

▼

What you get from both costume and gesture is an inner awakening. As aristocrats your gestures must be so assured you can do them with restraint. Our bodies are crippled. We do calisthenics. We do aerobics. Our bodies are healthy. What we really need is to find the *esthetic* body — and we do that through restrained gesture and control. Think again about the waltz.

You think I'm some deluded idolator of the lost age of privilege, that I long for the monarchy. Not so. I'm teaching you to behave outside of your limited experience, so that you'll have the power and control to portray anyone convincingly onstage. To play a king you must understand him, be him. And learning the aristocratic self-control will give you that power, that skill. The aristocracy, if nothing else, were great actors!

Let's have a few actors on stage arguing and an actor as a nobleman a rank above them enter and stop the argument simply with a motion of the head. With restrained gestures send some of the assembly to the right with the right hand, some to the left with the left hand. Then send the rest out the door with only your hand, head and a look.

▼

For next time, here are some actions I want you to illustrate with gestures in justified circumstances:

(a) "I defy you," which you express by pointing;

(b) "I give my life for my brother," which you express with arms outstretched; and,

(c) "I acknowledge the gods," which you express with a bow to the floor, your head touching it.

Here are some statements to make with justified gestures in circumstances, emphasizing the verbs:

(a) I present myself.

(b) I receive the crown.

(c) I rule here.

(d) I exalt what you believe in.

(e) I challenge you to believe me.

(f) I order you to stand.

(g) I summon the guards.

If you don't think it's working, do the gestures without the words. Let them feed you, then speak. Don't use false, melodramatic tones. If the gesture is restrained you'll hear the *word*. The gesture must never cover the word.

Remember, emotion is the cheapest commodity in the American theatre. Control is always more theatrically interesting. With control the words become clear.

Learn to deliver these three commands in justified circumstances:

> (a) "Bring him in."
> (b) "Bow your head."
> (c) "Kneel before your king."

As you prepare, bear in mind that the aristocrat performs even his duties *joyously*. Retain your self-esteem.

As aristocrats you should be able to say, with justification and not boastfulness, "Self! Self! Glorious!" If that which is glorious in the self is worthwhile, not merely selfish, take real pride in your self and your abilities.

Then, as actors, you should be able to proclaim, "You! Actors! Gielgud! Actor kings! Glorious!" And believe it — without acting.

THE ACTOR IS A WARRIOR

O ver the weeks we've been together I've been very aware that some of you sit out the class, watching, not working. I'm afraid you'll fade out. You must dare to work. Otherwise you'll fade into the crowd. You must grab the platform whenever you can. Don't hold back. Go forward!

That's one reason it pays to study the military mind. Another is that the military has been a theatre archetype for thousands of years. Yet another reason is it enables an actor to say, "I'm powerful" when you're young, when you're at an age when nobody will let you be powerful.

So assume the power. Be strong. Actors need a kind of aggression, a kind of inner force. Don't be only one-sided, sweet, nice, good. Get rid of being average. Find the killer in you.

You have grown up in a time that hates the military. You hate formality. You hate regimentation. The military is degenerated in our minds. We as a country are too passive. We don't see the army's epic size.

In Moscow during the Soviet period when a general entered a theatre or a restaurant his presence was overwhelming. He wore his medals. His uniform was full of embroidery. And he knew who he was. We haven't tolerated that kind of attitude in this country for many years.

General Patton had an excellent idea of the aristocratic military. He injected it into his troops. It helped him push through Germany like butter, with pride, with arrogance, with skill. His American soldiers weren't listless.

We have lost the sense that there's nothing stronger in a country than the army. For centuries it was the army that protected a country, protective of the people. It also protected tradition. Therefore it had a strong position in society.

Like the aristocracy, the army ascended in power with the downfall of the church. You must get an historical sense of the army because the military mind plays an important role in dramatic literature. You can't understand Coriolanus until you understand the military mind.

Some of the greatest speeches in Shakespeare are in *Henry V*, in which the king is rallying his troops before battle. An excellent speech to work on is, "Once more onto the breach, dear friends."

I'm always urging you to find ways to gain size. You must see these lines are full of strength, power and authority. The words come from God, through Shakespeare, to you.

Take the text and make it yours. The actor becomes richer as he makes the author's ideas his own. You are the conductor of the orchestra, not just a player. You cannot be weak inside. The actor must sense the power, the quality, the size of thinking in the text. If it doesn't mean anything to you, instinctively, you haven't got it. Or the part.

▼

We're going to do military exercises because the military energy should be your norm. A soldier is willing to die for his profession. You have to understand that kind of commitment. That's the norm for acting.

In the aristocracy the first son went into the army. The second son went into the navy. It's an archetype through history, but you don't have it in your culture. You don't have it in your blood.

We're going to do some exercises to understand the military body and mind. What we're working for is the automatic response, the sense that you're part of a force, a force ready to die to perpetuate and defend your country.

When we were examining the church we saw that, in resembling the pillars, the members of a religious order found power in order, in repetition. Here too we're not talking about individual power. We're talking about a group of men, following orders, unstoppable.

What is the military mind? It's a disciplined mind. A soldier follows commands without thinking. His is a mind going forward. It won't retreat. It goes forward because it must protect and defend.

Let's have the whole class onstage. Form yourselves into lines, evenly spaced lines, with each person in the line evenly spaced. Good. When I call out, "Attention!" snap your heels together and pull your stomach in and up. When I shout, "At ease," put your hands behind your back and stand with your feet apart. Now salute. All right, we're going to have a drill: Attention! At ease! Salute!

Let's march in place — left! right! left! right! Knees high!

Each row has a number, starting with the one on the left. Keep marching in place, but now, instead of "left! right!" shout out your numbers in sequence. Louder! Louder!

Get the feeling that you're part of a power moving forward, a relentless force. Nothing can stop it! You have to acquire a sense of that power and what it's used for. It's important to get the size, the largeness, the epic sense of a breed of men that controls and safeguards the country.

Say together, with this marching energy, "Once more unto the breach, dear friends, once more!" March!

One of the reasons actors study fencing is to teach them about aggression — how to advance, retreat, lunge — how to do it with elegance, with finesse. The foils enable you to fulfill your profession, to kill with honor and pride and even pleasure in the act.

You must physicalize your body. You must be willing to risk and dare. That's what the soldier does. That's what the actor does.

The actor and the military mind have more in common than you imagine. What's one of the most famous images of the military? Who do you think of immediately when you hear the words "military mind?" Napoleon. One reason you can easily visualize Napoleon is that he was extremely conscious of how he wanted to be remembered. He hired artists to paint him to impress his image not only on people he conquered but on posterity.

The artists he hired understood the EPIC SIZE of his power, the enjoyment of it, the joy of moving towards victory. In the paintings of Napoleon in battle you sense power and victory.

But what is the most memorable image you have of Napoleon? It may be the image of Napoleon on his white horse, because his body is very theatrical. His cape, his costume are theatrical. He understood that he had to project the sense of being somebody. He understood the import of being spectacularly decorated, ornamented.

The most famous image of Napoleon, however, is of him standing with his hand in his vest. This was how he posed for many of his portraits. Was it a random gesture? Of course not.

The important thing was that this gesture, which is how he wanted to be remembered, how he expressed his own power, was given to him by a Parisian actor. That actor shaped our understanding of one of the great men of history.

When you see paintings of Napoleon in battle, how are his men dressed? They wear uniforms of a brilliant red, blue and white. The uniforms designate rank, but, even more important, they're intensely theatrical. Even in the heat of battle they wore these dazzling uniforms. They never abandoned their sense of formality, their sense of tradition. Everyone and everything is regimented, thought through, but that doesn't mean it has to be drab. It's full of color.

There's a famous photograph of Winston Churchill taken shortly after World War II. He's wearing a highly decorated military uniform. It too is full of symbolism and theatricality. You look at Churchill and you think, "This earth, this realm, this scept'red isle, this England."

We have a similar tradition in America. What's one of our most famous military images? Washington crossing the Delaware. Washington stands in the prow of the boat. His hat has a very distinctive shape. It's really a crown. He wears a cloak. It's no different in shape from the cloak of Louis XIV. Did the general really pose like this in the rowboat? Was the painter an eyewitness? Does it matter? The image is what counts.

Generals know that it's good to bring theatre to warfare. It relieves the monotony of everyday routine.

Washington's costume declares he's going forward, going forward for a reason — to defend his whole country, to create a whole country.

▼

Let's think about one more warrior, in this case a 14-year-old girl who led the armies of France to great victories. Joan of Arc was fearless. How did she convey her fearlessness to men who were older and coarser than she was? She wore armor. It shocked them but they accepted her in a way they never would have had she worn her peasant clothes.

Did Joan impress the army of France because she was a great fencer? Did she lead them to victory over the English because she was a great pugilist? No, she led them with her mind, with her ideas — her ideas about France, her ideas about God. And with her presence, her sense of her own power.

Her weapon was her intelligence. With it she confronted the King of France. With it she taunted her enemies, the English military men who eventually conquered her. With this weapon she stood up to the lords of the Church, who feared her independence of mind.

With this weapon she could challenge them, call them liars. If they hadn't been afraid of her they wouldn't have burned her. There was nothing "girlish" about Joan. What made her so formidable was her ability to think clearly and to convey her thoughts to thousands of men to will them to accept her as their commander. She may have been a peasant girl, but Shaw presents her with an aristocratic mind.

In Shaw's play she's an historically recognized figure. Shaw says she represents the peasants of the world. Shaw says the peasant knows the truth. The church lies. Shaw said, If you educate the masses, each man will want to become Prime Minister. Joan represents that class.

She also represents the truth that power comes from the size of an idea. Joan confronts the Church and says, "You lied." Her ideas enabled her to look at the jewels, the symbols of wealth and power her adversaries wore and say, "They won't work! They're lies!" They lacked the confidence in their costumes that she had. Joan of Arc had no fear. She's a very good model for you. She saw herself as a bearer of truth.

▼

You think of the military simply as fighters. You must see that historically the military defended not just countries but ideas. The purpose of an army may be to vanquish the enemy, to kill, but the military mind is not about senseless violence.

There are big causes behind the military. The Crusades are

about a certain understanding of civilization and its enemies. In one of the great speeches in *Henry V* Henry urges his men to fight for "Harry, England and St. George." In another speech he tells his men, most of whom are peasants, that by fighting alongside him they're his equal, a very powerful idea at a time when class meant far more than it does now. One of the king's lieutenants voices a wish that they had more soldiers. Henry rebukes him:

> O do not wish one more!
> Rather proclaim it, Westmoreland, through my host,
> That he which hath no stomach to this fight,
> Let him depart; his passport shall be made,
> And crowns for convoy put into his purse;
> We would not die in that man's company
> That fears his fellowship to die with us.
> This day is call'd the feast of Crispian:
> He that outlives this day, and comes safe home,
> Will stand a tip-toe when this day is nam'd,
> And rouse him at the name of Crispian.
> He that shall see this day, and live old age,
> Will yearly on the vigil feast his neighbors,
> And say, "Tomorrow is Saint Crispian."
> Then will he strip his sleeve and show his scars,
> And say, "These wounds I had on Crispin's day."
> Old men forget; yet all shall be forgot,
> But he'll remember with advantages
> What feats he did that day. Then shall our names,
> Familiar in his mouth as household words,
> Harry the King, Bedford and Exeter,
> Warwick and Talbot, Salisbury and Gloucester,
> Be in their flowing cups freshly remember'd.
> This story shall the good man teach his son;
> And Crispin Crispian shall ne'er go by,

From this day to the ending of the world,
But we in it shall be remembered'
We few, we happy few, we band of brothers;
For he today that sheds his blood with me
Shall be my brother; be he ne'er so vile
This day shall gentle his condition:
And gentlemen in England now a-bed
Shall think themselves accurs'd they were not here,
And hold their manhoods cheap while any speaks
That fought with us upon Saint Crispin's Day.

Winston Churchill told the English they were fighting to save Western Civilization. The great French national anthem, the "Marseillaise," is not about what a beautiful country France is. It's about shedding blood, and the shedding of blood isn't seen as a gruesome task. "*Le jour de gloire est arrive!*" (The day of glory has come!") The military mind is about *La Gloire*!

▼

Your job as actors is to understand the size of what you say, to understand what's beneath the word. To convey ideas is the histrionic job of the actor. He must convey ideas without mystery, but with life's truth. The actor must sense the power, the quality, the size of thinking. He must learn the *ideas* of the great writers, not just the lines! You aren't parrots.

You must also recognize the size even of things you take for granted. Probably you haven't recited the Pledge of Allegiance since you were in grade school, when you probably butchered the pronunciation. As an exercise in understanding the military mind, recite the Pledge of Allegiance as a military person, justified and in circumstances.

Another excercise to prepare is to sing "My Country, 'T'is of Thee" while you crawl over a battlefield. Create an obstacle you must overcome — while you're crawling and without stopping your singing.

Then put some boxes on the stage and divide into groups. In each group someone will be the leader and give the order to "charge" over the boxes while the enemy's firing at you. The others must follow him. One person in the group will have to carry the flag and sing "Let Freedom Ring!" as he makes his way across the battlefield.

I also want you to work on some texts that reflect the military mind — *Henry V, Cyrano de Bergerac, Saint Joan, Tiger at the Gates*. All these plays need inner size, but work on them primarily to study the rhythm of military speeches. The language has to be understood by the rhythm.

As Americans you think the other fellow can't understand you quickly. That's why there's a kind of laziness about your normal speech rhythms. Lazy speech reflects lazy thinking. Your language is not "taut" enough. It lazes around, has no bite. The military mind is precise. And it's quick. In battle there's no time for imprecision.

One more thing — you no doubt think the military mind is about anger. Anger is cheap. Take the anger out. It's not a substitute for thinking, for ideas, for words. Look at history. Invariably the victorious side is the one fighting for an idea. Not even the awesome might of America could defeat the North Vietnamese, because they believed in their cause, their idea.

STANISLAVSKI AND THE NEW REALISTIC DRAMA

Once Harold Clurman and I were in Paris at the same time. To me Harold was a savior. He had initiated the Group Theatre, of which I was a part. He had made a theatre to which I wanted to belong. Harold was the man who did the most to open up my talent and my mind, who helped me educate myself about plays. He gave significance to my life, my theatrical life.

In Paris Harold said, "You know, Stella, Stanislavski is here." By this time I'd heard a great deal about Stanislavski. I'd known people who were participating in the Stanislavski technique. I myself was part of the Group Theatre, where the technique was supposedly being used. But as an actress who had a great deal of experience elsewhere, I resented acting with some of the principles used at the Group Theatre.

Because of this I became a stranger. I excluded myself from the way they rehearsed, the way the plays were directed. All this was known to everyone. They knew I was against what was happening at the Group Theatre.

Harold also knew my feelings. He thought it a good idea for me to meet Mr. Stanislavski. But I was hesitant. The idea frightened me. I told Harold, "If I meet him, I'll have in me a sense he was represented at the Group Theatre in a way I didn't want."

In the end I accompanied Harold to Mr. Stanislavski's home. It was a small French apartment with a small French elevator. When Harold opened the door, there were a few people in the room. It was a small room, and in the far corner was Stanislavski. The moment of meeting him was such a shock to me that I didn't move. Harold went over and greeted him. With Stanislavski were his doctor, a friend and Olga Knipper, Chekhov's widow.

Madame Chekhova stood near the door with me and said, "You must go over and shake Mr. Stanislavski's hand." I looked at her and said, "No." She said, "You must." I said, "No, I mustn't," and I didn't. I stood, completely unable to move, forward or backward. I was paralyzed by the whole moment.

Within a short time he suggested we all go to the Champs-Elysees. When we got there, Mr. Stanislavski sat on a bench against a tree, and we sat around him. There was great laughter and gaiety, the intimacy and wittiness that actors have. I remember distinctly Stanislavski chiding Madame Chekhova and calling her a ham, and of course she laughed. He pretended to bully her, and she pretended to be stronger than he was. There was humor, and an absolute moment of ensemble, and the joy of being there.

Mr. Stanislavski spoke to everyone and perceived I was reticent. Naturally, he'd notice that, because he had the "eye." Nothing got past him. He finally turned to me and said, "Young lady, everybody has spoken to me but you."

That was the moment I looked at him, eye to eye. I heard myself saying, "Mr. Stanislavski, I loved the theatre until you came along, and now I hate it!" He looked at me a little longer and then said, "Well, then you must come to see me tomorrow."

That was the moment I remember best. We said goodbye, and I went to see Mr. Stanislavski the next day. I told him I was a practiced actress. He knew of my family: He knew because my father, Jacob P. Adler, had produced *The Living Corpse* by Leo Tolstoi before he, Stanislavski, had played it. Adler was the first one in the world to play it, and this, of course, was known by everyone. Stanislavski understood I was the daughter of Jacob P. Adler and Sara Adler, a theatrical family.

Stanislavski and I soon achieved the greatest closeness of director and actress, and very soon it was just actor and actress! We worked together for many, many weeks. In those periods, there were certain things he asked me to do. Particularly, he made clear that an actor must have an enormous imagination, uninhibited by self-consciousness. I understood he was very much an actor fed by the imagination. He explained the enormous importance of the imagination on the stage.

He explained in detail how important it was to use circumstances. He said *where* you are is what you are, and how you are, and what you can be. You're in a place that will feed you, give you strength, give you the ability to do whatever you want.

Mr. Stanislavski told me, very much actor to actress, how he had suffered when he played Ibsen's *An Enemy of the People*. He didn't know where to touch it. He said it was difficult for him, that Ibsen was difficult for him. He told me it took him ten years to find the part. While he was gathering the elements for a technique that would make acting easier, he found the answer to the problem he'd experienced as an actor throughout his life, especially while working on *An Enemy of the People*.

In one scene of the play Stanislavski's character talked to the people and asked them to do something. That was wrong. He said, "I had to speak to the *soul* of the people. If I could reach their *souls*, I could get somewhere." Ten years after Stanislavski originally played the role, the play was revived; the part was his and now he could play it.

▼

Stanislavski realized plays were being written that could no longer be acted in the traditional way. He knew he had to create a way in which these plays could be done. He had to achieve a technique that could be used for every possible style. He had to have the means at his disposal to create the size and stature of man, with control, discipline, good speech.

The plays he was dealing with, of Ibsen and Chekhov and Strindberg, are realism. They raise the question, What is real? On the simplest level, this cup is real. Reality is something you can see and touch.

But realism is also a technique, a craft. It's an art form that asks the actor to reach and then reveal the truth. Realism teaches us the idea of the play is the first consideration. You play the play and you play the character to reveal the author's idea. You never play yourself. The actor's aim is to serve the theatre, never himself.

The late 19th century plays Stanislavski was wrestling with dealt with social conditions, the life people then were living. In social realism the hero has vanished. There are no longer heroes and villains. Everybody's a hero. The author presented right ways and wrong ways to behave, and the audience has to choose its own truths.

The main objective of Realism is to overthrow the lies of public and private life. Realism deals with the middle class. It finds out why the middle class is infected with the disease of inherited values, that is, values received through gossip, through the church, through education, through government.

Realism gets at and uncovers the truth of the human being, of the middle class and its way of life. When you approach the style of Realism, which is written in prose, you must approach it as a poetic form. Realism is based in language, but you need training to get the real meaning of what's being said.

It's a huge transition to go from the aristocratic class or the military class to the middle class. The aristocratic mind and the military mind are about formality. The middle class mind is informal. The aristocrat plays out his life in palaces. The military acts on the battlefield. The middle class life takes place in the family. Napoleon posed for history. The middle class man isn't concerned with pomp or glory. He's not posing for eternity.

In Realism's family there's a lack of stuffiness, of bluster. You couldn't set Queen Elizabeth or Louis XIV down in a middle-class family. They're too big for the home.

What the Realistic playwright is often saying is that the family, despite its lack of pretention, despite what they think of as the simple honesty of their behavior, is far more complicated than the monarchy.

▼

In *A Doll's House* Ibsen says the whole family situation is false. This big truth is the key to Realism. It's much more complex than you think. You must dig down and get the key to every word.

The middle class lives with invalid inherited ideas. We've been handed lies. We're corrupted by external opinions. We quote "ideas," but aren't secure we're speaking our own truth or somebody else's. Truth comes within, not from other critics, politicians, educators, journalists.

Nora's struggling with the lies of middle-class family life: "You don't love me," she tells her husband. "You lied to me. You say you love me, but you don't." She begins to analyze how she's come to think as she does. She understands her father and her husband have imposed their opinions on her. She realizes that when she thinks differently from her father or her husband, she suppresses it. She isn't allowed to think or decide for herself.

When you understand this truth, Ibsen's words mean something. The truth is big — don't tear it down. We want to hear Mr. Ibsen, not you.

To understand Mr. Ibsen we need to understand everything we can about his characters, their professions, attitudes toward family, money, politics, sex, religion, education — everything. For the actor this means moving slowly. We don't get what we need simply by looking at the words. We have to understand the whole social situation. We have to understand the social conflicts the playwright is trying to illuminate.

Ibsen shows the middle class is involved with money. They're not involved with museums or cultural growth. We've left behind the class concerned with deep thoughts. We're among a class diseased with practicality and ambition. Shaw said that in his time the aristocracy had been materialized, the middle class vulgarized and the lower class brutalized.

The middle-class is both materialistic and vulgar. They're not concerned with ideas, with glory. The middle class is concerned with selling, with profitable exchanges. The middle class says, "I want something for what I'm giving you."

The middle class arose from industrialization. The middle class mind is about producing things to make money. To the middle class mind time isn't something to be savored but to be spent, exploited. It's easier and faster to phone than to write. It's faster to turn on an electric light than light a candle. It's faster to take the subway or a car than to hitch up the horse and carriage. In the middle-class world you mustn't dawdle. Time is money.

In the middle class world "things" came into being. Commodities. The aim had changed. The middle class was concerned with success. Things had to have resale value. That aim reduced or ignored everything else, particularly individual growth and art.

People were stimulated to want more things — cars, refrigerators. But it sold out the inner man. The age of industrialization, of capitalism swept through the minds, hearts and souls of people. To achieve the new aim, success, they gave up the best of themselves. Cashed in their souls.

The capitalist point of view has infiltrated everything, commodified everything. Ambition, success and monetary power are all. The curiosity to develop the mind, the soul was wiped out by industrialization.

The desire for pragmatical success doesn't produce a Winston Churchill. It doesn't produce culture. It produces men with training, men equipped to lead the country. But we're left without tradition. NONE!

This mentality produces a different *rhythm* of seeing. It's a way of seeing without value, without depth. It creates an impoverished society with warehouses bursting with goods.

▼

America once had a very wealthy upper class. J.P. Morgan, in the Panic of 1907, loaned the American government $100 million to save the economy. Eventually he profitted handsomely by it, but it was still a great gesture — to personally bail out a whole country's economy.

Morgan was a man with enough mind to talk to a king or queen. Like an aristocrat, he carefully selected the horses that drew his carriage. They were pure white. They had style. His coachman wore a formal hat. Morgan was shrewd, intelligent, powerful, and he had one thing in common with artists — he knew that he'd live in history.

It's not difficult to study the mentality of this American upper class, who shared with aristocrats a love of fine things. Look at the paintings of John Singer Sargent to see how they dressed, the way they carried themselves. Or go to the Frick Collection and imagine what it was like when Mr. and Mrs. Frick lived there, when the paintings were their household decorations. This American upper class lived in palaces. They weren't very different from Europe's aristocracy. The main difference was their money was not inherited. They made it. (In fact, as the European aristocracy declined, American millionaires bought out their inherited treasures. Think Citizen Kane.)

These people in their heyday had taste and style. We weren't always as sloppy as we are now. Sitting up, behaving, having a sense of tradition disappeared during the Thirties with the Depression, with the collapse of the economy. The pity is that the actor's grandeur went with it. The mass mediums of film and TV took over.

This upper-middle-class had an entirely different range of "things" than we do. They wore top hats. What are top hats made of? Felt, with a silk border. Can you carry them any-where? Do you wear them to the beach? No. You could only carry them or wear them in certain circumstances. Where does the top hat "sleep?" In its own box or on a special shelf. Do you buy them off a rack? No, you have them made for you. There is even a special way to clean them — you have to follow the nap. We are used to things that are frayed. Would you keep a frayed top hat? Never. It defeats the whole pur-pose.

The upper-middle-class-woman carried a fan. Fans were like jewels. They generally came from abroad and were embroi-dered. The fan had its own language. It spoke. If you did this with the fan (*she motions*), it was a way of saying, Don't approach me. If you did that, it meant, Come now. I once studied with a Japanese lady to learn the language of the fan, to learn how to control it with the wrist.

Upper-class men carried canes. You used a cane not just to walk but to point, to call out, to twirl, to part the curtains to see if it was raining.

The upper-middle-class had opera glasses. They were some-times kept in a woman's jewel box. They were made of pearls, of gold and silver. The whole world of the opera was in the glass-es. They had graciousness.

Upper-class men carried pocket watches. If you ask someone with a pocket watch what time it is he has to take it out of his pocket. He can't just look at his wrist. It consumes time to find out the time. The implication is that time doesn't really matter.

That's totally different from our understanding of time. It's totally different from our *rhythm* of understanding today.

▼

As an exercise to teach us the middle-class rhythm of seeing, to help us distinguish it from an aristocrat's rhythm or an actor's, I've placed some objects on three tables.

I want you to get up, one by one, look around, see something, go to it, name it, recognize it, see what its use is, then go on to the next thing, quickly. Tell me, this is a pencil: you write with it; a phone: you make phone calls with it; a book: you read it. There should be no emotional connection. Just a rapid recognition of things.

That's the middle-class way of seeing. Fast, without depth. Each thing has its use. Each of these things can be made by the millions.

The result is that "things" lose their quality. Nothing feeds us. So we go to the money. How much did it cost? The telephone needs that rhythm. The camera uses that rhythm. Snap! Why paint something?

If we see that fast, with that rhythm, we have no dimensions. We cannot *think* in that rhythm. So we live in a society where things don't feed us. The culture of looking and seeing is more highly developed in other countries. Seeing in this way isn't American. We evaluate things for their usefulness.

But there's a way to look at even utilitarian objects in depth. The manufactured bottle has enough to give you two ways of looking at it. In America soda used to come in bottles. Now it comes in cans. In France they produce bottles of dark, smokey green. The bottom has a space for sediment to settle. The label is full of bright colors and a certain amount of reading matter. It's for wine, not Coca-Cola.

We should all spend fifteen minutes a day, less time than we give ourselves for exercise or jogging, working in this way, quietly, to give "things" value.

▼

You're industrialized, which deprives you of a sense of self. You've even gotten to the point of saying, "It's stylish to be nothing." Because of the quick surface acceptance of everything, you've lost something. You live your life with no value but the monetary.

Christmas is now all about buying and selling. We accept this. People are delighted when Christmas comes, but they have no idea what Christmas is. The symbol, the creche, has been left out. We lose the meaning of our lives.

Look at this table. It's black. It has no quality. The legs on the tables at Versailles were full of decoration. These legs are — a stab! They stand like prisoners about to be shot. You accept it. You don't know why it's made you so empty. This studio room says absolutely nothing. It's made to service you without *feeding* you.

As an actor you have to find a way to analyze the outside world to give it value. Trust me, it's there. You must be fed from the outside. If you feed only from yourself, you're pathological. There's no life where there's nothing outside. You must take time with things — to be nourished by them, not merely serviced.

A very good exercise to cultivate this sensibility is to sell something over the phone. It can be anything — vitamin pills, French lessons, a magazine subscription.

You'll understand the middle-class rhythm simply from pushing the telephone buttons. It was necessary to invent the push-button phone because dialing wasted so much time. Your rhythm is dictated by the technological society — fast! The machines are important to you. You need to be redesigned to accommodate them. Or you'll be discontinued. Look at your desk — the computer, the electric pencil sharpener, the electronic calculator. Is there an electronic vase? Yes! The screen saver. Digital flowers.

What does "to sell" mean? It means everything you sell has to *be* saleable. It's a way of looking at objects. Can I sell it? The more important the product is, the less you are.

In selling over the phone you don't know anybody you talk to. It forces you to neutralize your voice. You *mechanize* your voice. You're a zero in the structure.

A couple of years ago I sent a telegram to Robert Brustein. I thought my telegram was full of life. Then the operator read it back to me — with no feeling. She had de-personalized the words, drained them of meaning. Your culture has digitized words, stripped them of meaning, of history, of artistry. Words are numbers, preferably with dollar signs in front.

While you're selling on the phone, use as many props as possible. You live in a society where more than one thing is always happening. When you go to a movie you have popcorn in one hand, a Coke in the other. You have no concentration. You're modern by *not* concentrating. Or by concentrating on something electric that's doing it for you. That's the problem with mechanization — the machines do the living now, not us. All we can do is watch. There's nothing left to lift the spirit. So we go to psychologists.

A sign of our emptiness is our passivity, our indolence. We spend a lot of time waiting for something to happen. We express our impatience by tapping our feet, by drumming our fingers on a tabletop, by rubbing our hands together, by twisting a ring on our finger. All this is the body saying, "I'm doing nothing. I'm bored."

This is a good way to physicalize the American middle-class, of displaying the running engines we've all become. We're people who need to hurry, to speed up. But sometimes life stops us — we hit a traffic light. So we wait. And fidget.

And spin our wheels.

The practical man isn't a man of spiritual quiet. He's constantly doing something. He's incapable of being "laid back." However, you pay a price for practicality — even if nothing is happening, you keep going, going. Like that little battery-powered bunny.

The middle-class also keeps talking, talking. The talk isn't really *about* anything. It's as ready-made as the things they talk about — cars, TVs, VCRs, stocks. It just spills out, mass produced and cheap.

In fact this kind of character would be hard for you to play, this absolute American way of life. The interesting thing is that nobody here is practical. Your whole tendency is not to merge with the American rhythm. You feel withdrawn, even isolated. So it's interesting to bring you to the truth — that you shouldn't feel guilty if, as actors, you feel withdrawn.

We have to distinguish between the practical and the ambitious. They have many similarities but their aims are different. The practical doesn't include art forms. The practical brings everything "down to earth," to the level of "facts."

The ambitious doesn't pull things down. It involves "size." It involves something beyond Me. Ambitions may imply powerful, historical values as well as contemporary ones. The accumulation of power, in the aristocratic sense, meant the continuation of values, to go on and on, after you. It meant the establishment of museums and libraries.

The practical man says, "I'll drink this cup of coffee. Then I'll throw it out." The ambitious man says, "I want to drink out of Limoges cups." Morgan was an ambitious man. His ambition had size.

It's not bad to be ambitious. I once was ambitious to learn Italian. So what did I do? I got up early to study the textbook. I took lessons. I went to Italian restaurants to speak with the waiters. I kept doing, doing, doing every day. If you were to show my ambition in a play it would take the form of rushing to a lesson or talking eagerly to a waiter.

A student of mine was ambitious to play the violin. While he practiced his scales he kept setting the metronome faster and faster and faster as a way to make each finger independent, firm and secure. He played each measure over and over. At the end of four months he'd mastered the piece he wanted to play at a recital. In a play you'd show him running back to his room to practice. You'd show him doing things with the violin.

Can you find ambition in yourself? Remember, you cannot reduce any character to one element. It's not ambitious to take care of the garden.

Vladimir Horowitz was an extraordinary pianist, but he was also ambitious. What did he do to achieve that inhuman mastery? When he spoke to people who weren't in his musical world he used a side of himself that was childish, not to waste his musical intelligence. If he read the *Times*, he didn't go to the stock page. In a play you'd show him at the piano, not sipping coffee.

The difference between the practical and the ambitious is illustrated in Clifford Odets' play *Golden Boy*. The ambitious side of the character wants to play the violin, wants to become a musician. The practical part of him wants fame and fortune. So he becomes a prize fighter.

Ambition always leads to something bigger than being practical. Practicality doesn't involve the soul. How practical is it to play the E string over and over on your violin? Becoming a star in Hollywood is practical. Wanting to act in the plays of Eugene O'Neill is ambitious. There's a certain difference in attitude.

▼

Implicit in many plays about the middle-class is a sense of loss, of disillusionment. Middle-class life holds out a certain promise and then lets you down. All the running, all the acquiring doesn't really get you anywhere. Biff Loman rejects his father's values. His father believed in America, in the American way of life. He boasted that he "opened up the North" for his company. He was a nice guy. You can go far if you're well liked, he tells his son.

But Willy gets laid off, and Biff sees his father's values didn't work. America gave out the wrong hopes. It said to be a salesman was a form of glory. But it wasn't true. Willy was fired. Don't reduce it to a boy disillusioned with his father. It's the loss of America.

Willy won't accept that the American, the Jeffersonian dream is over. But Biff experiences the infinite aloneness of the American who doesn't want "the American way of life." It's an epic aloneness. He sees that unless you can be part of the system you can do nothing but buy another house. You're stranded. Capitalism gives you money but not peace. It's not a life of accomplishment.

The author's saying there must be some other kind of life we can create in this country besides work, success, money. Most of us are caught in this fruitless cycle. The artist has a way out. He's compensated by his joy in his work. But he's excluded from the middle-class.

Arthur Miller doesn't give Biff a real way of life by having him run away from success-oriented America. Being a farmer will not give him success. In Realism, in dealing with the middle-class, you won't get an answer. The audience must make up its own mind.

PORTRAYING CLASS ON STAGE

D on't be a stranger to anything in life. When you play a character you must see what you have in common with that character, but you must never stop there. This is especially true in the last of the archetypes we'll study, the peasant.

Where do you find the body of the peasant? You can do it partly by observation, if you know where to look. You can find it from locale, from travel. But a very good way to understand the peasant is to look at the Breughel painting "The Wedding Dance."

The first thing you must notice is its absolute gaeity. The picture gives you nothing about poverty, about being harrassed or persecuted. There's nothing about nervous tension. They're free, gay and full of optimism.

There's nothing graceful about their dancing, but it's enormously joyful. There's a sense of harmony and unity. They know how to be together in a way that gives each other joy. That's something we've lost.

This is genuinely a picture of *community*. In the world of these peasants no man needs to feel alone, isolated or different. They have a common structure, which unites them.

Notice that it's not a world that lacks conventions. Both men and women wear hats. They seem to have no practical necessity. The hats for both sexes are purely decorative. The peasants don't have much money — that we know — but they still dress with a sense of ornament.

Obviously they don't have the formality of the aristocrat or even the middle-class, but there's nothing slovenly or messy about them. Although they've probably made an effort to look festive for the wedding, there's a sense that they could dash from the party to serve their masters if necessary.

In Breughel's painting of farmers working hay fields you get an almost encyclopedic view of what people do. Everybody knows how to do something. There are no amateurs. They're surrounded by trees. The've got the land. They've got everything that make them happy.

To play the peasant, you must give yourself over fully, muscularly, to the type. You're connected with life in all its animal ways, its dirt, its sexuality. There's a boldness, a fullness to the peasant. His choices are limited — he eats, drinks, sleeps, fornicates, dances. Sex is good. Life is good and unashamed.

His relationship with life is physical. You must *do*, not say. There's no delicacy. The attitude toward death is not so frightened. The peasant is simple, direct. There's a spontaneity and a lack of restraint.

But it would be wrong to suggest that the peasant is so coarse he's incapable of finer understanding. Let's take another Flemish painting, a 16th century "Adoration of the Magi" by Hieronymus Bosch. Note the setting — a manger, which has an elegant sound, but it's simply what we would call a barn. Does that make it less joyful? Not at all.

The Holy Family is surrounded by farm implements, which isn't how they're depicted in many portraits of the Nativity, but that only adds to the feeling of intimacy.

You have to cleanse your minds from thinking somebody else is "low." The peasant is different. He wears different clothes. He has less money. But he's not low. In fact for many years fashion houses have imitated peasant clothes from all over the world because they're colorful and comfortable. We hide ourselves with clothes, but they wear clothes that don't hide themselves. The essential thing about peasant clothes is they're exuberant.

One reason the peasant is joyful is he has something he can never lose — the earth. His roots are there. That's the cosmic truth he understands. He knows man is tied to the earth.

I'm talking about the European peasant, possibly the European peasant of today, certainly the European peasant of only a century ago, when the English novelist Thomas Hardy, in *Return of the Native*, has one of his characters, a city person, observe that when you go to the country you regain your sense of life as something to be enjoyed rather than merely endured.

We don't have that here. America got mixed up. We weren't tied to anything. Until it was too late the American farmer saw his land as something to develop and sell. It was a commodity, not a legacy.

The peasant's joy comes from everything the earth provides — plants, vegetables, animals. In Breughel's paintings you have a sense of everything growing together, dancing together. There's a sense of fullness and openness. The earth doesn't hide. Nothing's hidden. They have a sense of freedom about their bodies.

In European peasant life everybody makes a family. In poor sections of Italy any child belongs to any woman. If a child is lost or dirty, any woman takes in the child, comforts him, washes him off and puts him back. So it's not *your* family or *my* family. It's more, we're *all* family. There's an experiential *togetherness*.

The peasant hasn't lost the animal nature of man and woman. An animal doesn't say, "Let's get an introduction." In the animal world there's no destiny — man and woman will get together in some way. It will take a lot off your mind to know there's no destiny.

All this is not to say peasants are mindless, that their life is painless. If you're playing a peasant, it's a good idea not to have a full set of teeth.

Much of our life is concerned with protection from the elements. The peasant lives in direct contact with them. He shares his circumstances with the earth and he's constantly exposed to nature — clouds, rain, mud, sunshine. He doesn't need sex manuals. The sex he enjoys is like animals mating. It has the qualities of spring and joy.

I can't stress enough that the peasant is not low class. They have a way of life that's not ours, but it's not inferior. They have places to live on the land granted to them by the landowners. They don't worry about mortgages. They don't belong to trade unions. They're not plumbers. They don't think in terms of the hourly rate. They think of doing the job they have to do.

They're comfortable on the earth. They're not slobs, not bums, not poor! They accept life and death as a part of each other and a part of the earth. They accept the earth. Forget dirtyness when you play the peasant. For him it's not dirt — it's earth. You have to understand the difference. For the peasant you must have part of the earth on you. You must be open.

A good exercise for understanding the peasant is to dig for potatoes. You must create the circumstances — is the earth wet or dry? Forget your own restraint. Justify having earth on every part of you.

What we said about the aristocrat is also true about the peasant. What you wear affects who you are. The peasant wears wooden shoes and sturdy boots. Look at Van Gogh's painting of peasant boots. This is a world in which nothing is made to be discarded. Everything has value. Nothing is old — or rotten. Man wore and outwore these boots. They're as much part of the working class as the apron is part of the maid.

▼

There's a part of you that you can use as you develop a character. The actress who plays Anna Christie in O'Neill's play doesn't have to work as a whore to understand the character. She may know what it is to keep a contract. A whore is a professional. She has a detachment about her work. She's out to make money. There must be a ruthlessness about her. When she fulfills a contract, she doesn't sell the whole store. She gives only what was agreed.

But your understanding of a character has to go beyond your own life. When Marlon Brando was working on the role of Stanley Kowalski in Tennessee Williams' *A Streetcar Named Desire*, he used Van Gogh's painting of the boots to help him understand the character. He saw Kowalski as a peasant who'd come to the city and was broken by it. "Very good, Marlon," I said. "But how do you make it doable? How do you show him broken?"

He developed a slouch. Which turned out to be more famous than Van Gogh's boots.

▼

The peasant class we've been looking at is rural. There's also a tradition of the working class, which is urban. The working class in America has gone through many phases. But someone living in it cannot understand it.

There is no way to talk about the contemporary working class. In America it no longer exists in its purest form. So we'll have to go back in history for the spirit of the working class before trade unionism made it into a business.

The working class derives from the European peasant class, small farm workers from the country, before we had modern cities and high-rise buildings. They were a class that went right back to the land. So the place was the land and the land became a city.

This class is built upon the basic principle of working from the land. It's impossible to think of this historical working community without thinking of their games and music. Working-class people often played an instrument — the harmonica or the guitar. As time went on they adapted themselves to other instruments, other games.

The workingman comes from a community of earth and work. The workingman had a sense of self, a sense of power. He respected himself and said, "I'll work till I die!" He was a man, nothing bent, nothing crooked, nothing broken.

He moved very freely, very deliberately. He wasn't a slob or a bum. He lived on his land in his log house with a fence around him. He lived the way a man could live, the best way he could in his circumstances. Whether he had heavy machinery or a wooden plow to mend, he'd deal with it. He did his job, an honest man's work.

You can't call the workingman in America today the working-class man. It's a tradition and was handed down from father to son. It's different now.

▼

Class distinctions were absolutely without compromise in other periods. In our own time there are no social aspirations. We have democratized all the classes. This is not to say we have eliminated classes. It's just harder to see them. But seeing them clearly is part of your job as actors.

You have to know the class you're playing. We're a democratic country. We have a moneyed class, an upper moneyed class. We have a lower moneyed class. We don't really have what you call a working class. The doorman at my building owns three properties in the best part of New York and his new car is parked in front all the time. He's my doorman, you see. *I* don't have three properties. Not that there aren't poor doormen, only that the classes are no longer absolute. They're fluid, elastic.

When you work on Tennessee Williams you have to understand all these distinctions. You also have to understand the South. The South built itself up as if it were Greece. It had its own aristocracy, its own values, its own way of living. Its men and women behaved a hundred million times differently than you, thought differently, acted differently and understood ideas differently. They have nothing to do with your education or your life. But Tennessee is played all over the world. I heard last year in Moscow there were seven productions of his plays.

In the South they had a mixture of classes, and, as you know, they had the cotton industry, which meant millions of black people working the plantations. That's where most of the activity is going to take place. Certainly most of the drama.

If you had a dollar in 1700 you could buy a half acre. As a matter of fact when people first came over everybody received fifty acres — every stranger. It was a big country, a lot of land and nothing to work with. If you look at the map it looks as if the whole world is the South. It's enormously large.

It was difficult, all these classes who came, from the working class to the nobility. It was also where the English transported their criminals. So you get the aristocracy in the beginning and the criminal, working his way up, both creating a culture.

If you're brought up in a culture with slaves and proprietors, it's very different from the one you know. And some of the people had plantations as palatial as the homes of the King of France. The palatial quality in the South we've never touched in the North, but that's what they wanted to build and what many did build.

Now we get to the Civil War. We all think that that was a nice war because the North won and we freed the slaves. That's romantic thinking. What Tennessee, who was brought up in the South, understands is the Reconstruction period. For the South Reconstruction was for the Yankee to get the South's cotton, produce it and make money. The North wanted the South's money, earned out of exploiting the Negro population, and fought on that principle. They wanted to make the South into another big Northern industry.

The South didn't feel beaten by the North. They didn't act as if they were beaten. In Tennessee Williams you see the unconquerable quality of the South.

I was invited to judge some one-act plays at the University of North Carolina. Each night I saw three one-act plays and I was astonished. This was not a very long time ago, but every play was about the Civil War, and the South, and in every play the South won. In every play the hero was a soldier.

They understood the military temperament in the classic sense. The leaders of their army were gorgeous and behaved well and treated people well and loved their army, and the South loved leadership. We don't like leadership. We like humans. They worshipped their leaders, followed their leaders, imitated their leaders. And that's what gave them their aristocratic quality.

General Lee was elegant. You've never seen a man in uniform that made you worship a military leader. If you see Lee and the way he kept himself and then look at how Grant was dressed, you understand the North and the South. The South built up people to be aristocratic in behavior and appearance. They built families that were respected. Family life was respected in the South.

In the South men understood by the way another man was dressed what class he belonged to, whether they were genteel or poor whites. You can't recognize that in New York. Nobody knows who the man next to him is by appearance. Now, all over the United States we dress alike — shorts and sweaters or a T-shirt and dungarees. A homogenized look.

In the South Williams writes about you see at least four classes — poor whites, the aristocracy, the working class and slaves. That's a lot to learn. For them as well as you. They had to keep it straight or pay the consequences. And so do you, as actors portraying them.

You may ask what do I mean by "gentleman?" You have the outside behavior of a gentleman even in the working class. That's very important to know because you'll appreciate why the original semblance changes in the social situation. They respected the uniform. They wanted that to continue. The whites, the poor whites, everybody wanted to continue the aristocracy of the generals as they grew older and as the Civil War receded.

They accumulated that kind of behavior and wanted people to lead them. An incredible nunber of Southern people were admired because of their behavior. They were dying and starving because they lost the war and the cotton prices plummeted. The acreage was sold off piece by piece. But the Southerner was and behaved like a gentleman. And that's very Southern, and very much what Tennessee Williams deals with.

Southern men admired the deportment of other men. They imitated it. They were manly, courteous, careful, very courtly. Now the word courtly means: I bow and I'm not intimate. Never intimacy. They had a great courtliness and they had a sense of dignity whether they were poor or rich. They had a sense of comradeship.

This is what I'd like you to understand, that it was not according to money. It was the nature of their culture to have a nobleman's attitude toward himself — a good mind, an educated body, a very educated mind. You were very much looked up to if you had that. The poorer classes looked up to it, wanted it and imitated it.

What they did was the opposite of what we do. From their point of view we're still Yankees. The North meant money-grabbing, carpetbaggers, exploitation, lack of education, lack of honor, lack of integrity. That's what the North displayed, with a lot of rape for good measure, economic and physical. Get what you can. Get it for nothing or steal it. That was the North's ideal.

Whatever the North does is about money. We're money-minded, ignorant, bad-mannered, uneducated. How many people know that the North is almost bankrupt in these virtues?

The North said to the blacks, "You're free but you still have to work for nothing." I'm not speaking from a Southern point of view. I'm speaking more or less from Tennessee's point of view.

▼

At the beginning of the Second World War the South was impoverished, and that's in Tennessee's plays. When the land goes piece by piece, when the security of owning something goes completely, you get *A Streetcar Named Desire*. There was no work. There was complete collapse.

The poverty is so bad that in Tennessee's first plays people live in tenement houses in the worst possible way. In *The Glass Menagerie* the only way to get into the two-room flat is through the fire escape. Now you begin to estimate the poverty: there was no entrance to where they lived. In *Streetcar* the impoverished class intrudes on Stanley Kowalski's flat. You get people called Blanche Dubois and you see what poverty has done to her and her family.

She's exiled from the South because they sold everything and they went bankrupt and she goes from this job to there, and so you have the aristocrat of old times, educated in the South to be special, absolutely special, special to such a point they had to play a role in life.

The Southern woman's way of life was a mask. She found an affected speech. Even if she went to the drugstore she had to be this white woman who behaves in a white way. Even in poverty she maintained the mask of plantation life, and she hadn't a dime in her pocket. Not a dime.

The Southern woman was the center, she was the life-force.

She was superior to anybody because she could continue the upper class white children. The center of Southern life was the woman who continued the tradition of white children. This gave her a need and gave the men the need to be superior.

The men forced them to act a certain way, to be superior. They wanted purity in the woman. Purity meant, "I don't talk to anybody. I'm not intimate with anybody. I don't shake hands with anybody except my superior parents. I'm remote from intimacy." They had to give a performance of this false quality, to do it constantly so that it was *recognized* as a performance.

Blanche comes in, floating eyes and looking around and seeing she's in a poor white little lousy two-room flat. She's so startled by the poverty, she's so . . . frightened . . . She's destroyed immediately.

Most of you will have trouble understanding that. Did you all come with the Mayflower? No. You're all Poor White Trash. We have no lineage, and I want you to understand this. You can't judge characters in respect to your own middle-class life. You have to see them from their perspective, portray them from their perspective. Otherwise you'll only ever play you and your family. I want you to understand that in the American antebellum South there was a male who created a woman to be the mother of his white child and in that sense he had power and strength and she was artificially shaped by her purity.

I don't think anybody talks about purity any more, do you? Is anybody here pure?

The pull in Tennessee's woman is away from success and away from facing consequences. I don't think any woman today doesn't understand you have to grow older and have to be sick and have to fight the world. Tennesse's women don't face the ordinary problems of life. In *Streetcar* these absolute worst specimens of life come in Saturday night to play cards, and Blanche is busy seeing if she's properly dressed. Stanley thinks that's neurotic, and I think so too.

Does this clarify to some degree the role of man and the role of woman? The world of this play begins at a plantation that only the chateau of Louis XIV could equal, And then it goes bust. Complete bankruptcy forces the citizen to leave and go to other cities. They're no longer part of that great plantation, and in other cities they have to face the reality of small city life

Are we clear now about poverty and how difficult it is for the Southern mother who believes she has seventeen gentleman callers? You see she was surrounded with this whole glamour world of praise and they gave her so many flowers they cover the garden, as she remembers.

In *The Glass Menagerie* she has one person to call on her daughter, a lovely virgin, who is both crippled and incapable of functioning. For this one gentleman caller who makes, I think, ten dollars a month, who has no future ahead of him, who's stupid and vulgar — for him she puts on all these clothes she had when she was a girl.

Now I think that's a tremendous culture, to put on for a cab driver the dress you were married in.

▼

In most of the plays you'll work on there'll be conflict. Two ways of life contending. It's your privilege and duty as an actor to lift both to their highest levels, to give them size, to enhance and not to diminish the theme of the playwright.

When you've worked hard enough on these principles, with confidence you can say you've learned a technique of acting that will stay with you. If it doesn't manifest itself at once, it will appear later.

If, as actors, you've done your homework, there's no cause to be humble or apologetic in applying to agents or directors or producers. You've done the grinding work demanded by your profession, and they haven't. You'll begin to act when you can forget your technique — when it is so securely inside you that you need not call upon it consciously. By opening up, you allow it to happen to you.

Free your talent and let it work. By the miracle of *non*-acting you accomplish your aim. When you most succeed, you do so by seeming not to act at all.

But even success is a transient goal. No actor ever feels he is forever good. Even when he works well and knows it's good, he feels tomorrow it won't be.

The actor has a built-in broken heart, which helps him to understand, but doesn't help him win. There's no actor who looks like a banker at the end of life. He looks distinguished, but not as if he's won. The actor pays a price, and that price is his heart.

AFTERWORD

For several millenia the Jews sought truth in sacred texts. In this century they have looked elsewhere — in millenarian politics, in the return to the Promised Land, and, for a small but vocal group, in the theatre.

Does it seem odd to begin a discussion of the technique lectures of Stella Adler on a theological level? It shouldn't. It should be clear from the simplest perusal of these lectures that she was not engaged in transmitting a mere mechanical approach to how to conduct oneself on stage.

Stella Adler had an exalted idea of the theatre. As she stresses constantly, it was an idea of the theatre that was 2,000 years old. There was no doubt in her mind that the theatre was a vehicle for discovering and disseminating truth. Over and over again she stresses that the theatre is about ideas.

To be worthy of this idea of theatre, to be worthy merely to stand on the stage, the student must prepare himself with as much dedication (though happily without the self-abnegation) of a novice preparing for the priesthood.

That may explain why she could occasionally be so severe with her students — she was not running a vocational school. Her idea of vocation had nothing to do with "job training." It was in every sense a higher calling, and she had little patience with those who did not share her lofty notions of the art they had come to her to learn.

Stella Adler's understanding of the theatre was shaped by three men — her father, Jacob P. Adler, one of the towering stars of the Yiddish theatre; her husband and colleague, Harold Clurman, the founder and spiritual leader of the Group Theater (and later a husband of hers); and Konstantin Stanislavski, the Russian actor who was the first to understand the special problems of the modern theatre and to formulate a technique to deal with them.

To her father she owed a profound knowledge of a working life in the theatre. He was not only the star of his company but the manager of it. Living with him gave her an opportunity to study every aspect of the theatre.

She might have had this experience even if her father had been a journeyman actor, but he was a great one. She was fond of pointing out that Stanislavski was well aware that her father had played the leading role in Leo Tolstoy's *The Living Corpse* before he did.

She stressed how, from their earliest childhood, her father had inculcated in her and her siblings, several of whom also went on the stage, the habits and behavior essential to an actor. In fact, fourteen of the Adler clan would eventually enter the theatre world in some capacity, in effect creating an important American theatrical dynasty.

Although her relationship with Harold Clurman was complex and stormy, she never failed to acknowledge her debt to him as a teacher, as a man with a profound understanding of theatre. She knew he was a visionary. It was his almost spiritual belief in the power of theatre that had led to the formation of the Group Theater. In the bleak days of the Depression, the Group was a beacon for many who imagined the theatre might play a far more powerful role in American life than merely providing diversion.

In *Real Life*, Wendy Smith's book about the Group Theater, she makes clear that it was Clurman who gave the often beleaguered Group members their inspiration, their sense of mission.

For Stella Adler to join the Group involved financial sacrifice and the curtailment of an already burgeoning commercial career — she did it because she shared Clurman's vision.

It is no accident that many of those involved with the Group were Jewish. It was a way for them to fulfill the messianic aspirations they no longer associated with the faith of their fathers.

It also seems no accident that the longest lasting effect of the Group was pedagogical. The Group produced many fine actors, a number of great directors, but the most influential result of its short but turbulent life (the Group barely lasted a decade) was the creation of some of the most respected acting teachers of the postwar period — Lee Strasberg, Sanford Meisner, Robert Lewis, and, of course, Stella Adler.

The fierce disputes they had with each other over the interpretation of Stanislavski's teaching, the techniques they had developed for interpreting dramatic texts can easily be seen as a secular outgrowth of thousands of years of wrangling over knotty questions in the Bible and the Talmud.

A century earlier they might all have been sages to whom gifted students would have been sent from all over Eastern Europe to study the mysteries of the Word of God. The intensity, the intellect they brought to the study of dramatic technique and dramatic literature suggested that, in their eyes, these were not lesser objects for their passionate devotion.

As for the third of her influences, Stanislavski, Stella Adler was very proud that, of all those who made a living imparting the techniques he had developed, she was the only one who had actually studied with him.

From the start of her association with the Group she had had deep misgivings about the way Strasberg, who had been, with Clurman and Cheryl Crawford, one of its co-founders, was interpreting Stanislavski's methods.

Unlike many of the members of the Group, who were beginners, she had already had many years of stage experience in her parents' company and was thus better able to judge the practical value — or lack thereof — of Strasberg's approach.

Until she actually met Stanislavski she had no way of knowing how Strasberg had altered his ideas. She only knew that she could not accept what Strasberg was rigidly imparting to the largely blank slates of the Group members.

"Mr. Stanislavski, I loved the theatre until you came along," she told him when they met in Paris. "And now I hate it."

After a moment's pause, Stanislavski insisted she must come to see him so he could set her straight about his techniques. For the next several months she studied with him daily. What she learned confirmed that what Strasberg had been teaching the Group was his own method, not Stanislavski's.

The issue on which they were most sharply divided was that of emotional memory, an idea Stanislavski had developed early in his thinking about what acting is but had subordinated to other ideas as time went on.

For Strasberg the re-creation of experienced emotions was at the heart of the actor's task. For Adler — and, she stressed, for Stanislavski — the imagination must take the lead. The emotional experiences of the actor are not the same as those of the character he plays. Intelligence and imagination lead the actor into the mind of his character. Acting, Adler emphasized, is an effort that goes out toward the audience, not something merely self-referential.

For Adler acting was in actions. Actions, she said, elicit emotions both in the actor and the audience. If the actor understands the nature of the actions he performs he is helping the audience understand its own behavior more deeply.

The emphasis on doing rather than feeling makes the Adler approach more practical. It is reasonable, she — and Stanislavski — asserted, to expect the actor to be able to perform actions; it is not reasonable to expect him to conjure up emotions.

The emphasis on *doing* also has a very Old Testament quality. What has been seen as the legalistic tone of the Pentateuch stems from its insistence that the deity is not an abstraction. He is a living force who makes specific demands — Thou shalt do this, thou shalt not do that. One affirms one's faith not merely in prayer or meditation but in very specific actions, like leaving part of one's field unharvested so the poor can gather it.

One such injunction was, "Thou shalt not seethe a kid in its mother's milk." Inherent in this command is a sense that all living things must be approached with an awareness that they are sacred. The rabbis quibbled over how to fulfill this commandment for centuries. Their wrangling led to the laws of what is kosher and what is not. By forbidding altogether the mixing of meat and milk they made certain a kid would never be seethed in its mother's milk.

The notion that actions have profound undercurrents and that the nature of an action is worth quibbling over both underlie Adler's approach to acting. In this sense her teaching was a secular version of the interpretive battles in which Jews have been engaged for millenia. So were her disputes with the other Group alumni who became teachers.

Given the personalities of Strasberg and Adler, it is odd that Strasberg should have been the better known. Adler was intensely theatrical. She was a beautiful woman and presented herself grandly. The composer Richard Adler recalled that when he was a young man in the '40s she was invariably the most striking person in the room, the person toward whom all eyes were drawn, even if Chaplin were there.

The respect she commanded was enormous. In the '70s, long after he had been her student, Marlon Brando, who had personally created the T-shirt and jeans as the uniform of the modern actor, surprised a journalist by appearing in a suit and tie. When the journalist asked why he was so dressed up, he explained he was having lunch with Stella Adler.

Curiously, despite the flamboyance of her public persona, Stella was inexperienced at self-promotion. In the mid-Sixties both she and Strasberg were invited to Moscow to observe the ongoing work of Stanislavski's creation, the Moscow Art Theatre. When she returned Stella took the teachers of her school to dinner to tell them what she had learned. On *his* return, Strasberg held a press conference.

▼

This book grows out of Stella Adler's relationship with Glenn Young, the publisher of Applause Books. Young felt his rapport with her stemmed from their discussions, over dinner, over tea, of the plays of Ibsen, Strindberg and Chekhov.

"My interest was always in the interstices of the text, certain moments, certain propensities of the characters," Young recalled. "I think she was intrigued by someone who had a specific not a general interest in these plays, in the subatomic level of these plays. We got along very well on that molecular level.

"A turning point in our relationship came when I had the temerity to offer an opinion of her book on acting. I told her I believed she deserved a better book than the one that was allowed to appear under her name.

"Anyone who knew Stella knew the richness, the Baroque quality of her mind, the arrogance of her reach into many fields at once. If anyone knew that the theater was the converging point of history, philosophy, economics, psychology, color and light, it was Stella Adler. The quality of her thought could not be reduced. It could never be refined either. It was always going to be something robust.

"There was something extravagant about her disposition. She wanted you to be extravagant. She offered you the right of passage into this intellectual extravagance, and the book that had been produced was, to my mind, the antithesis of that.

"It was a pale, reductive, mechanical book in which all the adventure and all the fire had been depleted and expunged. All those flames had been tamed.

"I think she'd been surrounded by people who told her how much they loved that book. I was probably the first person to say it might not be the best testament to her legacy.

"At one point she summoned me to her apartment near the Metropolitan Museum on Fifth Avenue. She showed me into a small room with notebooks surrounding each wall. 'Darling, I have my whole life in this small room. I want you to spend time in this room and tell me what to do with my life.'

"Anybody who knew Stella knew she could be at the same time very coy and make requests like a prim commandant.

"With that she gave me the key to her apartment and left for California. Over the summer I went into that room for a few hours at a time. I sat without taking many notes. I read notebook after notebook of her work. Many of these notes were repetitious. Many of them seemed to be reincarnations of themselves. But even in those reincarnated moments there would be a spark of surprise, a new example, a new exception she would offer.

"Shortly after she returned from California, where she had been teaching, she summoned me once again and asked for my counsel.

"At this point I knew the only way to represent Stella Adler properly was to project her in her fullest, most visceral persona. I knew that one could never properly feel the force of her ideas unless one heard fully the force of her voice, and that became my most abiding sense of how Stella's work should be captured.

"One needed the life between the synapses of the thought to ring true. In order to inculcate her wisdom and insight, one would have to inject a dose of Stella's personality and the largeness of her spirit and the magnaminity of her spirit and even what could sometimes be the gradiosity of her spirit.. That was the spirit that was missing from the theater and from the New York teaching scene.

"When it came time to publish this very book I had no question but that the mandate would be to hear the voice of Stella Adler in every line. The greatest compliment that could be paid this book would be the day someone calls for the performing rights to one of the chapters.

"When Stella Adler walked into a classroom someone of spiritual aristocracy walked in. I wanted the reader to understand why some of the most cynical, crazy, irreverent young people who are inevitably the artists and actors in New York would, without hesitation, all rise and applaud when Stella Adler walked into the classroom."

▼

This was the mandate Glenn Young gave me — to convey not only the literal teaching of Stella Adler, but the tone in which it was imparted.

There was nothing dispassionate about her classroom manner — when I interviewed her in 1983 she said she regarded teaching as a form of acting, and, judging by the class I attended, which began with a moving eulogy for the just deceased Tennessee Williams, indeed it was.

In many of the lectures I listened to on audiotape there was a dramatic structure — there would be a formal introduction, a deepening involvement in what was being taught, a sudden escalation into emotionalism, often involving terrifying screaming at the students, followed by a cooling down, and, almost as a gesture of reparation, an unexpected tone of intimacy.

The preceding chapters are based on a series of audiotapes of her technique lectures in 1983, a 1985 manuscript by Stuart Little, a subsequent reduction of that manuscript, a set of transcriptions of her lectures by Marjorie Loggia and Milton Justice, various other unidentified transcriptions and numerous notebooks on her lectures. There is also material from the presentation of her technique in a book published in 1988.

My own understanding of her technique is based on an invaluable course of acting lessons I took from one of her students, Ivan Kronenfeld. I am also grateful to Ron Burrus, who worked closely with her for many years, for allowing me to watch his classes.

This is not a conventional "how-to" book. Stella Adler, I think, would have been insulted by such an approach. For her the art of acting was inseparable from a philosophy about the world in which the actor functions. That world, she sees — as an Old Testament prophet might have seen — is a fallen world.

As she puts it in her remarks about the aristocratic archetype, "The leveling down of the European man is our greatest danger. This is the prospect that depresses us. Today we see nothing that wants to become greater. We suspect that all goes ever downward, becoming thinner, more sleazy, smarter, cozier, more ordinary, more indifferent. Exactly here lies the crisis. With the fear of man, we have also lost the love of man — reverence for him, hope in him. The human prospect wearies us. What is the current nihilism if it is not that? We are tired of man."

Faced with this crisis, she sees the actor playing a redemptive role. He can remind the audience of who they are and what they can be. In *To the Finland Station* Edmund Wilson notes that Marx's view of the workers as a potentially world-saving class stemmed from a mistaken identification of the proletariat with the Jews. Adler made a comparable identification in her claims for the actor.

Adler's observations about "the leveling down of European man" might seem more appropriate to a lecture on philosophy than an acting class, but it is indicative of her approach that she saw the theatre as an arena for thought, not simply a form of show business.

▼

Whatever her students imagined, she was preparing them not for careers in television or movies but for their eventual confrontation with the "sacred texts" of dramatic literature. She assumed their goal was to play King Lear or Hedda Gabler, not Lance and Cherie on some soap opera.

The principles she taught them would stand them in good stead regardless of the texts to which they were applied, but her vision, like that of Clurman, and, equally important, like that of Stanislavski, was of the actor not as an entertainer, not as a commercial entity, but as a bearer of poetry and truth.

Colleen Dewhurst once recalled that when, as a young actress, she had gone to study with Adler and Clurman she was surprised that they wanted their students to play kings and queens. Until then, Dewhurst said, she and her fellow students had not thought to look beyond the kitchen — needless to say, the working class kitchen — as the venue for great drama. That remains too often true.

Such myopia makes it all the more essential that Stella Adler's voice, in all its complexity — its vehement passion, its sometimes comic disdain, its often hyperbolic anger, its down-to-earth wisdom and its undeniably patriarchal grandeur — must continue to be heard.

— HOWARD KISSEL

THE COLLECTED WORKS OF HAROLD CLURMAN

Six Decades of Commentary on Theatre, Dance, Music, Film, Arts, Letters and Politics

edited by Marjorie Loggia and Glenn Young

"... RUSH OUT AND BUY *THE COLLECTED WORKS OF HAROLD CLURMAN* ... Editors Marjorie Loggia and Glenn Young have assembled a monumental helping of his work ... **THIS IS A BOOK TO LIVE WITH;** picking it up at random is like going to the theater with Clurman and then sitting down with him in a good bistro for some exhilarating talk. This is a very big book, but Clurman was a very big figure."

JACK KROLL, *Newsweek*

"**THE BOOK SWEEPS ACROSS THE 20TH CENTURY,** offering a panoply of theater in Clurman's time ... **IT RESONATES WITH PASSION.**"

MEL GUSSOW, *The New York Times*

CLOTH •ISBN 1-55783-132-7 PAPER • ISBN 1-55783-264-1